GIFTS FOR BABY

GIFTS FOR BABY

30 simple crafting projects to welcome the new arrival

CATHERINE WORAM

photography by POLLY WREFORD

RYLAND
PETERS
& SMALL

LONDON NEW YORK

First published in the United States
in 2007 by Ryland Peters & Small, Inc
519 Broadway, 5th Floor
New York, NY 10012

www.rylandpeters.com

10 9 8 7 6 5 4 3 2 1

ISBN-10: 1-84597-458-1
ISBN-13: 978-1-84597-458-9

Library of Congress Cataloging-in-
Publication Data has been applied for.

Printed and bound in China.

SENIOR DESIGNER Sonya Nathoo
COMMISSIONING EDITOR Annabel Morgan
LOCATION RESEARCH Emily Westlake
PRODUCTION Gordana Simakovic
PUBLISHING DIRECTOR Alison Starling

STYLIST Catherine Woram

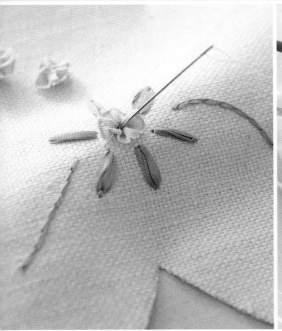

contents

introduction

Handcrafting something special for a new baby is a very tangible way of demonstrating your love for the new arrival and, indeed, his or her parents. When a gift is made by hand, it's somehow more meaningful both for the maker and for the lucky recipient. Many such items become precious keepsakes, ones that will be cherished by future generations as well as our own.

This book contains 30 gorgeous projects designed especially for new babies. The projects range from the simple—a painted rattle, perhaps—to the more elaborate, such as an embroidered patchwork blanket. We've divided the gifts into three different sections. In *For Baby*, there are adorable items for the new arrival to wear or play with, from cute buttoned shoes to a cuddly bunny. In *For the Nursery*, you will find decorative pieces such as a crib mobile and pretty picture frames. *Keepsakes* is packed with ideas for gifts that are sure to become family heirlooms, including a painted toybox and a cross-stitched picture. The final section, *Perfect Presentation*, offers suggestions for gorgeous gift wrap and unique cards.

The projects are made using materials that are readily available from craft stores and notions departments. Each one is illustrated with step-by-step instructions, while the techniques section clearly demonstrates all the necessary basic sewing skills. Whether you are an accomplished crafter or an enthusiastic novice, you will find projects to suit your level of expertise.

I hope you will enjoy looking at, making, and giving these delightful projects, and that many of them are destined to become future heirlooms for your friends and family to enjoy!

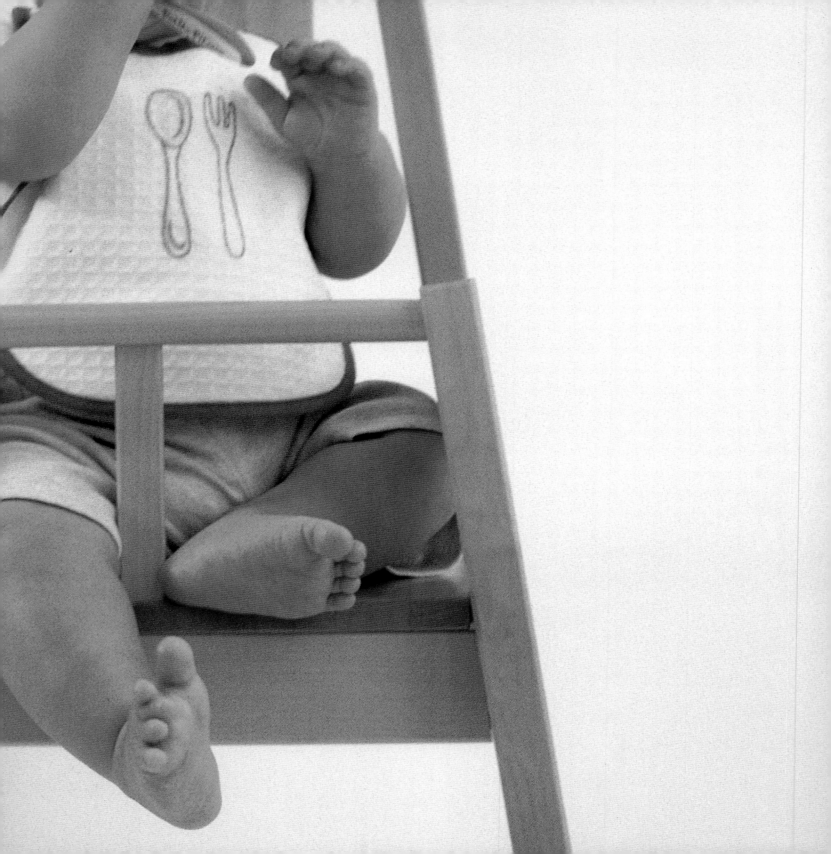

FOR BABY

soft wool toys

This beautifully soft teddy and bunny are made from a fine wool fabric and decorated with simple embroidery in delicate pastel shades. They are filled with soft synthetic-fiber stuffing, making them lightweight and perfect for baby to cuddle.

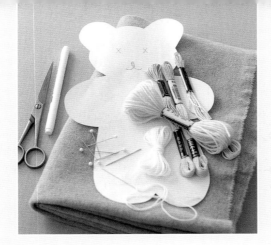

WHAT YOU WILL NEED
paper for template • 12in (30cm)
square piece of wool fabric per toy
• pencil • scissors • pins • fabric
marker pen • embroidery thread
• tapestry yarn (or two-ply knitting yarn)
• needle • synthetic-fiber stuffing

create a template Trace the teddy
(or bunny) template on page 119 onto a
piece of plain paper and cut it out. Mark the
position of the eyes, nose, and decorative
stitching on the paper, if desired.

cut out fabric Fold the fabric in half and pin the paper template
to the fabric. Carefully cut around the teddy (or bunny) shape using
sharp scissors. Use the fabric marker pen to mark the position of the
eyes, nose, and decorative stitching on one of the body shapes. If the
fabric you are using has a tendency to fray, you may find it easier
to draw around the template with the marker and then work the
embroidery before cutting out the shape, to prevent fraying.

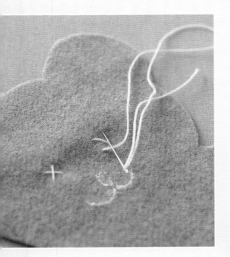

embroider eyes and nose Using embroidery thread, work two crosses for the eyes
in the position indicated on the template. Work the nose in small straight stitches, then
work the lower part of the nose using tiny chain stitches (see Techniques, page 115).

decorate the body The decorative
sprig motif stitching on the teddy's lower
body is worked in lazy daisy stitch grouped
in clusters of three. The sprigs are worked
in pale yellow, pink, and blue cotton
embroidery floss using two strands
of thread at a time.

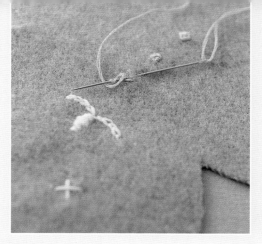

embroider french knots

Using the yellow, pink, and blue embroidery thread, work three small French knots (see Techniques, page 114) just below the teddy's face.

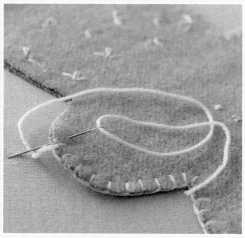

stitch together Position the two pieces of fabric with wrong sides together and baste in place around the edges. Now start to stitch the bear together all the way around the edges, using small blanket stitches (see Techniques, page 112). Stitch approximately ½in (1cm) apart, using a single strand of yarn (we used 2-ply knitting yarn, which is very fine). Remember to leave an opening of approximately 2in (5cm), so you can stuff the bear.

add stuffing Fill the bear with stuffing, using a pencil or knitting needle to push it gently into the ears, arms, and feet. Insert enough stuffing to make the toy plump and easy to hold, but not too firm or overstuffed.

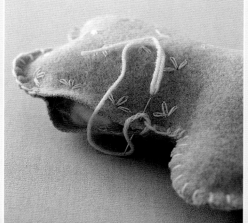

finishing Once all the stuffing has been inserted, hold the edges of the fabric together and continue to work the blanket stitch along the opening until the edges are completely closed (it may be easier to baste the opening closed before continuing with the blanket stitch).

hints and tips

• This cute bear was cut from a piece of cuddly lavender-colored wool and has been decorated with the same gentle pastel embroidery threads.

• By increasing or reducing the size of the template (see page 119) on a photocopier, you could make a whole family of bears (perhaps a normal-sized mommy, a bigger daddy, and a smaller baby bear) in different colors.

bunny beanie hat

This cute little hat is made from soft cotton
T-shirt fabric and features contrasting "bunny"
ears. The embroidered nose and whiskers give
it a fun twist. The cotton fabric is the ideal choice
for newborn babies, as it is lightweight and soft.

WHAT YOU WILL NEED

paper for template • pencil • scissors • 12in (30cm) white cotton T-shirt fabric, 44in (137m) wide • 8in (20cm) beige T-shirt fabric for ears • pins • needle • sewing thread • sewing machine • fabric pen • beige embroidery thread

create templates Trace the hat and ear templates on page 117 onto a piece of plain paper and cut them out. Remember to mark the notch for the ear position on the paper pattern.

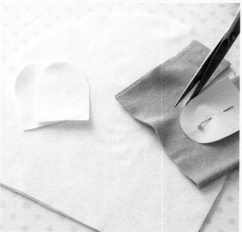

cut out fabric Fold the fabric in half and pin the paper hat pattern to the fabric. Carefully cut around this shape using sharp scissors. Snip a small triangular notch in the fabric to indicate where the ears will go. Pin the ear pattern to a folded piece of white fabric and cut two ear shapes from this fabric. Now use the same pattern to cut two ear shapes from the beige fabric.

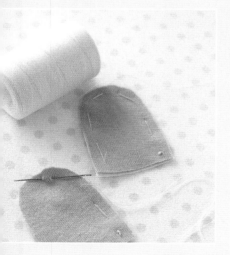

make the ears With right sides together, baste one white and one beige cotton ear piece together. Leave the flat bottom edge of the ear unstitched, for turning right side out. Repeat with the other ear. Machine stitch around both ears and trim. Clip the curved edges and turn right side out.

baste hat together Pinch a pleat in the center of each ear piece and stitch in place by hand. Place one hat piece right side up. Lay each ear on the marked position on the hat and pin in place. Lay the other hat piece on top, right side down, sandwiching the ears between the two layers of fabric. Baste together, leaving the bottom edge open.

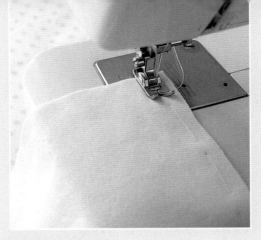

machine stitch Place the hat on the sewing machine and stitch around the basted edges of the fabric. If you have a stretch stitch on your machine, it is best to use this stitch, although it can be done with a standard straight stitch.

make the hem Fold a 1½in (4cm) hem toward the inside of the hat and pin in place. Press in place and baste along the folded edge. Machine stitch in place, using a zigzag or stretch stitch.

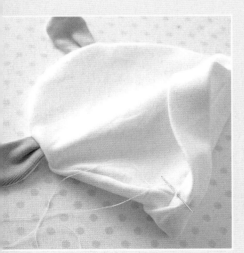

fold the brim Trim the curved edges of the hat and turn right side out. Roll the edges of the fabric between your fingers to flatten them. Fold up 1in (2.5cm) from the bottom of the hat to make the brim and press in place. Just inside the brim, sew a few stitches on each side of the hat to hold the brim to the side seams so it can't roll down.

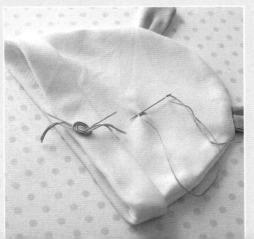

finishing Using a fabric pen, mark the eyes and nose as shown on the template. Work a few straight stitches for the eyes, using two strands of floss. For the nose, cut three 3in (7cm) strands of thread and knot in the center. Knot again, then trim so the whiskers are 1in (2.5cm) long on each side. Stitch to the center of the brim to finish.

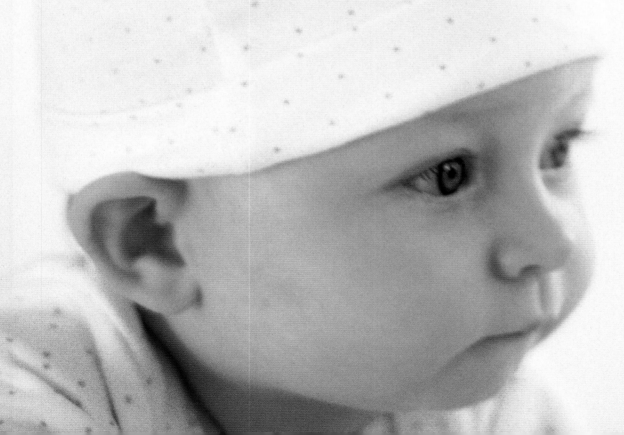

hints and tips

If you have bought a pretty onesie for a new baby, why not personalize the gift by making a bunny hat to match? We bought a matching shirt in the same polka-dotted cotton fabric as the onesie, and cut it up to make a hat. Contrasting pink cotton was used for the bunny ears. Cotton onesies and shirts are perfect for making hats, as the cotton is very fine and soft against baby's skin.

wooden teething ring

Softest cotton velour in pale pastel colors and a wooden curtain ring are used to create this adorable teething ring. The ears are made from contrasting fabric, while the eyes and nose are embroidered in straight and chain stitches.

WHAT YOU WILL NEED

paper for template • pencil • scissors
• 6in (15cm) piece cream velour, 44in
(137cm) wide • smaller piece pink
velour for ears • fabric pen • beige
embroidery thread • needle • pins
• sewing machine • synthetic-fiber
stuffing • bell or rattle, if desired
• wooden curtain ring

create templates Trace the templates on page 117 onto paper and cut them out. Pin to the cream velour and cut out one strap, one face, two back sections, and two ears. Cut two ears from the pink velour. With right sides together, baste one cream ear to one pink ear.

embroider face Sew the first ear together on a sewing machine, leaving the bottom edge open. Turn right side out. Repeat the basting and stitching with the other ear. Now, using a fabric pen, draw the ears and nose on the face of the rabbit. Work the nose in tiny chain stitch using two strands of embroidery floss. Make a few straight stitches to work the two eyes on the rabbit face.

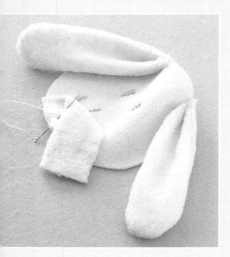

attach ears and strap Fold the strap section in half lengthwise and stitch down one side using a sewing machine. Turn right side out and stitch the strap by hand to the bottom of the rabbit's face, in line with the nose. Pinch the ear sections to form a pleat. Place each one, pink side down, on the rabbit's face. Pin, then stitch in place.

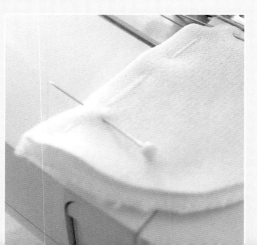

stitch the back section Pin the back sections together, right sides facing. Baste together along the straight edge. Using a sewing machine, stitch in ¾in (1.5cm) from each outside edge, leaving a gap in the middle. Leave the basting in place.

join front and back pieces Tuck the ears and strap into the middle of the front section. Lay the back section on top with right sides together, sandwiching the ears and strap between the two layers of fabric. Baste the pieces of fabric together then machine stitch all around the edges.

turn right side out Using scissors, trim and notch the curved edges of the fabric. Clip the basting stitches that held the opening in the back section together. Now turn the bunny head right side out by carefully pulling the ears and straps through the opening. Roll the curved edges of the fabric gently between your fingers to flatten the edges.

add stuffing Use a knitting needle or a bodkin to push the stuffing inside the rabbit. The toy should be plump, but not overstuffed. If desired, insert a bell or rattle right in the center of the stuffing. Hand stitch the back together using whipstitch. Use two strands of floss and make sure the opening cannot come undone.

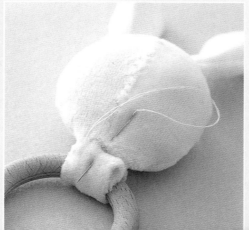

stitch to ring Fold the strap of the teething ring around the wooden curtain ring as firmly as possible. Tuck the raw end inside the strap to conceal it. Now stitch the ring to the strap, using whipstitch to hold it together securely.

hints and tips

Leftover fabric from the bunny beanie (see page 14) or
the knotted pixie hat (see page 22) would be perfect for this
project. You could also try substituting white plastic curtain
rings for the wooden ones shown here.

knotted pixie hat

The jaunty knot on the top of this cute-as-a-button cotton terrycloth hat gives it a playful pixie effect. The tiny embroidered French knots are a dainty finishing touch.

WHAT YOU WILL NEED

paper for template • pencil • scissors • pins • 12in (30cm) stretch terrycloth fabric, 44in (137cm) wide • sewing machine • needle • white embroidery thread

create the template Trace the hat template on page 116 onto a piece of plain paper and cut it out. Fold the fabric in half, pin the template to the fabric and cut around it using scissors.

stitch hat pieces together With right sides together, baste the hat sections to each other, leaving the straight bottom edge open. Stitch using a sewing machine. Trim and clip the curved edges of the fabric (you will need to trim approximately ¼in (5mm) of fabric from the top pointed section so it turns inside out easily). Turn right side out and roll the curved edges of fabric between your fingers to flatten the edges. Tie a knot in the top section of the hat.

make the brim Fold a ¾in (1.5cm) hem to the outside of the hat and baste in place. Stitch using zigzag stitch or stretch stitch on your sewing machine. Now fold the hem of the hat up approximately 1in (2.5cm) to form a brim, and secure in place by making several stitches by hand at the side seams inside the fold of the brim.

embroider french knots To finish the hat, use white embroidery thread to work French knots approximately ¾in (1.5cm) apart all around the brim of the hat (see Techniques, page 114).

miniature mary janes

The perfect gift for a baby girl, these adorable button-up shoes have a contrast lining and a flower-shaped mother-of-pearl button.

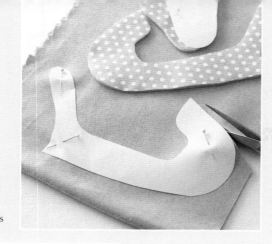

WHAT YOU WILL NEED

paper for template • pencil • scissors • 12in (30cm) iron-on foam interfacing • 12in (30cm) wool fabric • 12in (30cm) cotton polka-dot fabric • 2yds. (2m) cream bias binding, ¾in (1.5cm) wide • pins • needle • sewing machine • thread • two plastic snap fasteners • two mother-of-pearl buttons

create templates Trace the templates on page 116 onto a piece of plain paper and cut them out. Iron the foam interfacing to the wrong side of the polka-dot lining fabric and let it cool. Now cut two shoe sections and two soles from both the wool fabric and the lining fabric.

stitch together With wrong sides together, stitch each of the shoe sections to the lining sections by hand, using tiny, flat whipstitch. Repeat for each of the soles. Fold in ⅛in (3mm) all the way down each side of the the bias binding and press with a hot iron. Now fold the bias binding in half, wrong side to wrong side, so the folded edges meet, and press. Let it cool.

baste bias binding Baste the bias binding all the way around both the shoe sections, folding the raw ends in to prevent them from fraying. Repeat for the sole sections. Use your fingers to manipulate the bias binding around the curved edges of the shapes. Using an iron, press flat when the basting is complete.

stitch bias binding Using a sewing machine and matching sewing thread, topstitch the bias binding to the shoe. Repeat for the soles. If necessary, iron the bias binding flat, to remove any creases caused during sewing.

form shoe Curve the shoe sections around to form a shoe shape, so the bottom of the strap piece meets the other end as shown. Starting approximately ¾in (1.5cm) up from the bottom, stitch by hand to secure in place. Double the thread to make the stitching stronger.

attach soles Now place the sole section inside the base of the shoe, with the narrower end facing the back. Using cross stitch, begin sewing the shoe and the sole together, starting from the center back of the shoe and continuing all around the whole shoe (see Techniques, page 113).

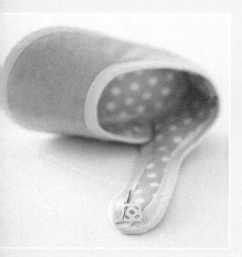

sew on fastener Sew a plastic snap fastener to the inside end of the shoe strap by hand. Now sew the corresponding piece of the fastener to the side of the shoe (the exact positions for the fasteners are marked on the shoe templates).

add button To finish, sew a pretty button to the outside of the shoe strap to cover the stitches of the snap fastener.

hints and tips

• Softest sky-blue gingham is used for the inner and
outer sections of these shoes, which are finished with
star-shaped buttons

• Use soft fleece fabric for a cozy winter shoe,
or add further decoration in the shape of silk ribbon
embroidery (as shown on the heart pillow on page 92).

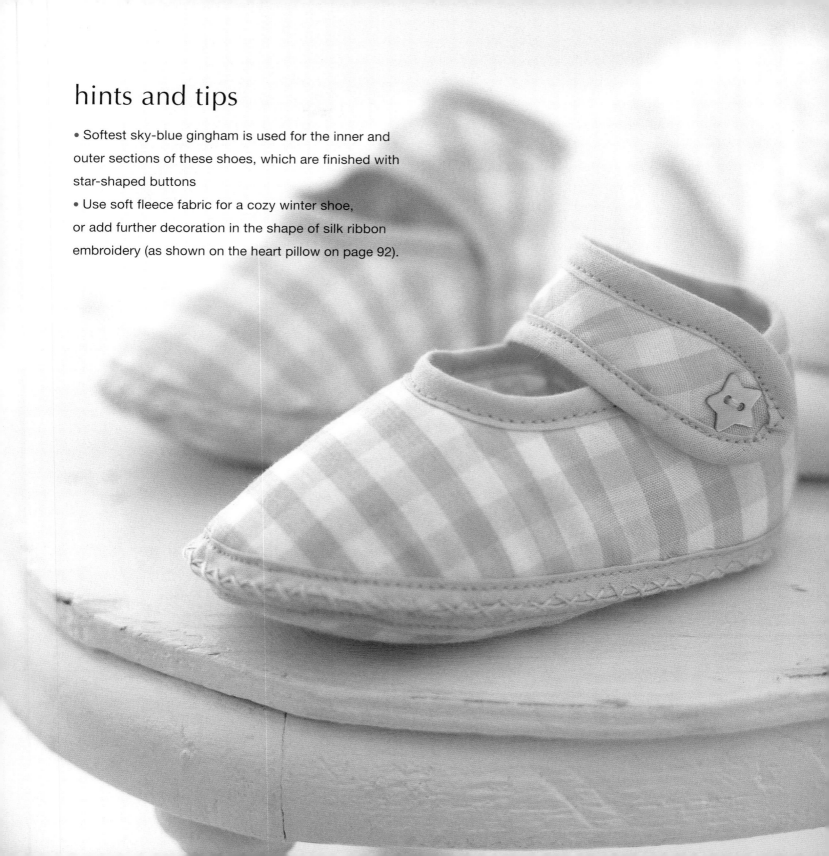

best-dressed bib

This gorgeous traditional-style bib has an old-fashioned charm all of its own. Made from plain white linen, it has been embroidered with a simple baby's bottle motif and decorated with a dainty silk bow.

WHAT YOU WILL NEED

paper for template • pencil • ¼ yd. (25cm) linen fabric, 44in (137cm) wide • pins • scissors • black pen • fabric pen • needle • embroidery thread in four colors • 4in (10cm) narrow silk ribbon • 1¾ yds. (1.5m) bias binding, ¾in (1.5cm) wide • thread to match bias binding • sewing machine

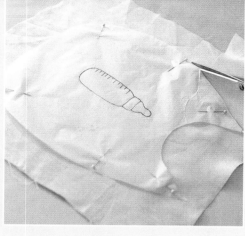

create a template Trace the bib template on page 118 onto a piece of plain paper. Carefully draw the bottle motif onto the template. Cut out the template and pin it to the fabric. Using sharp scissors, cut out two bib shapes.

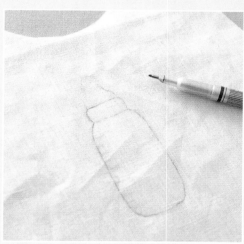

trace motif Draw over the bottle motif on the tracing paper using a black pen, so it is visible through the linen fabric. Lay the tracing paper under the linen bib shape, and carefully trace over the bottle shape with a fabric pen.

embroider motif Work the bottle motif using chain stitch (see Techniques, page 115). We used different colored embroidery thread for the bottle, neck, and nipple. Use two strands of embroidery floss, to prevent the chain stitching from becoming too thick.

finish embroidery Use a single strand of gray embroidery floss to work simple straight stitches to mark the measuring levels on the bottle (as indicated on the template). When you have finished embroidering the bottle, press the embroidery from the back of the bib.

sew on ribbon bow Make a tiny bow using the narrow silk ribbon and stitch it by hand to the bottom of the bottle top. Cut the ends of the ribbon diagonally to prevent them from fraying.

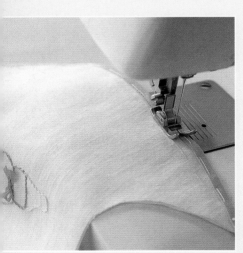

baste bib together Place the two bib pieces with wrong sides together, and baste around the edges of the bib. Leave the neck open so you can turn the bib right side out when you have finished. Fold a ⅛in (3mm) hem all the way down each side of the bias binding, and press. Now fold the bias binding in half, wrong side to wrong side, so the folded edges meet, and press. Cut a 24in (60cm) length from one end of the bias binding, and set aside.

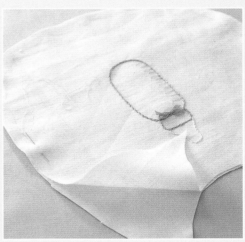

attach bias binding Sandwich the raw edges of the bib between the folded bias binding all around the outside edge of the bib, and baste in place. Leave the neck of the bib uncovered. Topstitch in place around the outside of the bib using a sewing machine.

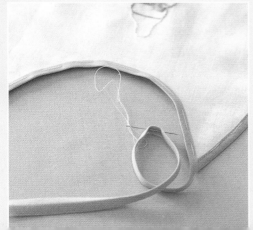

finish off Take the 24in (60cm) piece of bias binding. Mark the center of the bias binding with a pin. Pin this to the center of the neck of the bib. Baste the bias binding around the neck, covering the raw ends of the bias binding that runs around the bib. Topstitch in place on a sewing machine to finish.

hints and tips

• To make this bib more practical and durable
at feeding time, add a layer of plastic lining fabric
between the two layers of linen.
• You can see an alternative "silver spoon" motif
on the bib on page 8 (see Templates, page 118).
This was worked in gray embroidery floss on
white cotton seersucker.

painted rattle

All babies love the sound of rattles, and the
action of grabbing, holding, or shaking a rattle
is great for developing motor skills. Decorate a
rattle in pretty pastel shades or vibrant hues
to create a fun gift baby will love.

WHAT YOU WILL NEED

plain wooden rattle • non-toxic paints in two different shades • two fine paintbrushes • soft white pencil • water-based non-toxic acrylic varnish

gather materials
Decant small amounts of the paint into glass dishes. It may also help to have an object (like a small tumbler) in which you can stand the rattle while the paint is drying.

apply undercoat
Apply an undercoat to the rattle to provide a base key for the color paint. Next, apply one or two coats of the main color and let it dry thoroughly between each coat.

draw on design in pencil
Use the white pencil to draw heart motifs (or similar) on the rattle, each one approximately ¾in (2cm) apart.

finish painting
Use a fine paintbrush to fill in the heart motifs. Paint the outline first, then fill in the center. A second coat of paint may be necessary for the hearts to achieve denser coverage. Once completely dry, apply one or two coats of water-based acrylic varnish to finish.

fabric blocks

Pretty vintage-style fabrics were used to make these fabric blocks, which can be used as a plaything or as decorative accessories for the nursery. You can insert a tiny bell or rattle inside each block to add an extra dimension to this toy.

WHAT YOU WILL NEED

paper for template • pencil • scissors
• foam cube 3 x 3in (78 x 78mm)
• bell or rattle insert • pins • 6 fabric
pieces, each 4in (10cm) square, for
each cube • needle • matching
sewing thread • sewing machine

create a template Draw a 4 x 4in (10 x 10cm) square onto paper to create a template (the blocks can be larger or smaller—reduce or enlarge the size of the template and adjust the size of the foam block accordingly). Most foam suppliers will cut cubes to the required size.

insert bell or rattle Using a pair of sharp scissors, pierce a hole in the cube and insert the bell or rattle carefully into the center. Close the opening by covering it with a piece of tape.

cut out fabric squares Each cube requires six fabric squares. Pin the paper template to the fabric and cut out one square. Now cut out five further squares from different patterned designs.

baste together With right sides together, baste two fabric squares along one edge, allowing a seam of ½in (1cm). Baste the next square to the edge of the previous square, and repeat until you have a strip of four squares.

stitch squares Machine stitch along the basted edges of the squares, then baste the two raw ends of the strip, right sides together, to form a cube shape. Machine stitch the last edge, and trim and notch the corners of each seam. Press the seams open.

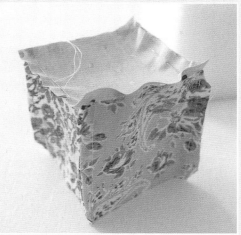

add top and bottom Stand the fabric cube on a flat surface, wrong side out, and pin one of the remaining fabric squares, right side down, to the top edges of the cube. Baste in place, carefully folding the fabric at the corners (you may have to trim the corners to facilitate this). Machine stitch in place around all four sides. Baste, then machine stitch, the last fabric square to the bottom of the cube along two sides only. Now turn the cube right side out.

insert foam block Carefully ease the foam block into the fabric, making sure not to rip any stitches. Work the foam into the corners of the cube so it sits properly within the cover. You may wish to iron the fabric with a warm iron when the cube has been inserted.

finishing Fold the two open edges of the top square to the sides of the block. Hold or pin the edges of the fabric together and use whipstitch to close the opening neatly and securely.

hints and tips

For a baby boy, we made fabric blocks in a cute sailing-boat fabric. Cowboy or soldier designs would also work well.

snug hooded towel

Cuddly bath towels with hoods are
the perfect addition to any layette. This
design in plain white with an embroidered
crown motif would make a gorgeous and
practical gift for a baby boy or girl.

WHAT YOU WILL NEED

1yd. (1m) white terrycloth, 44in (137cm) wide • scissors • paper for template • pencil • pins • 5yds. (4m) yellow bias binding • orange thread • sewing machine • 8in (20cm) square yellow fabric for crown motif • 8in (20cm) square fusible web • needle • orange embroidery thread

cut out Cut a square of terrycloth 36 x 36in (90 x 90cm), rounding off the corners of the square. Use one corner as a guide to create a triangular template for the hood. Cut it out, pin it to the left-over terrycloth, and cut out the hood. Trace the crown on page 118 onto paper and cut it out.

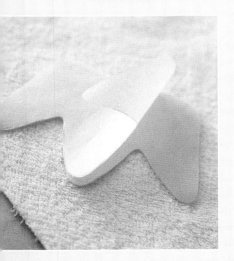

add bias binding Cut a length of bias binding to fit the bottom straight edge of the hood section. Fold a $\frac{1}{8}$in (3mm) hem all the way down each side of the bias binding, and press. Now fold the bias binding in half, wrong side to wrong side, so the folded edges meet, and press. Sandwich the hood edge between the folded bias binding and baste. Stitch in place using a sewing machine.

iron on motif Iron the fusible web to the wrong side of the yellow crown fabric. Place the crown template on the paper side of the web and draw around it. Cut out the shape. Peel off the backing paper and place the crown in the center of the hood section. Iron in place, following the manufacturer's instructions. Let it cool completely.

stitch motif Sew all the way around the crown motif using a zigzag stitch on the sewing machine. Repeat two or three times so that the stitching is dense. It is better to use a slightly looser stitch and repeat it several times, as a very close stitch tends to pucker the fabric.

embroider Using two strands of orange embroidery floss, work a row of seven French knots along the base of the crown motif (see Techniques, page 114). Now work a single French knot just above each point of the crown.

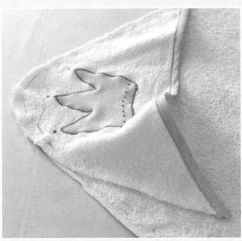

baste hood to towel Place the hood section on top of the towel, right side up. Make sure the curved corners are lined up. Now baste the hood section to the towel to hold it in place while stitching on the bias binding. Cut a length of bias binding 4yds. (3.7m) in length. Fold in a ⅛in (3mm) hem all the way down each side of the bias binding and press. Now fold the bias binding in half, wrong side to wrong side, so the folded edges meet, and press.

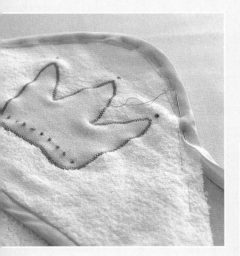

add bias binding to towel Baste the bias binding all the way around the edges of the towel, taking care to sandwich the edges of the towel and the hood section in between the bias binding. Use the fingers to manipulate the bias binding around the curved edges. Press flat with a hot iron.

finishing Topstitch around all the edges of the towel. Press the bias binding with an iron to flatten, if required.

hints and tips

• A blue crown and bias binding gives the towel a more boyish appeal.

• To make a washbag with a matching crown motif, follow the instructions for the laundry bag on page 58, but reduce the size of the bag to approximately 8 x 12in (20 x 30cm).

FOR THE NURSERY

heart crib decoration

This pretty chain of soft stuffed hearts makes a
dainty addition to any crib. The hearts are stuffed
with soft synthetic-fiber filling and decorated with
ribbon bows. Remember that all hanging toys and
decorations should be removed from the crib by
the time a baby can get up on its hands and knees.

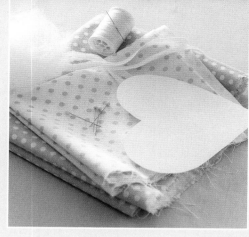

WHAT YOU WILL NEED

paper for template • pencil • scissors • pins • for each heart, 6in (15cm) square blue polka-dot fabric and 6in (15cm) square reverse polka-dot fabric • synthetic-fiber filling • 3yds. (2.7m) narrow cotton tape • matching sewing thread • needle

create a template Trace the heart template on page 118 onto a piece of plain paper and cut it out. Remember to mark the notch for the opening (for the stuffing) on the template.

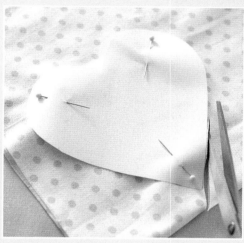

cut out fabric Pin the template to the fabric and cut two heart shapes per decoration. We used three blue polka-dot hearts and two white on blue polka-dot hearts for the decoration shown. Cut two tiny notches on the fabric to indicate the opening for the filling, which should be left open until the very end.

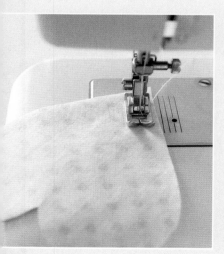

stitch hearts together With right sides together, stitch the heart shapes, leaving the opening for the stuffing as indicated on the template. Repeat for each of the five hearts used to make the decoration.

trim and notch edges Clip the curved edges of each heart so it lies flat when turned right side out. Turn right side out through the opening. Roll the edges of the fabric to flatten them, then press the heart shapes using an iron.

stuff hearts Use a knitting needle to push the synthetic stuffing into the heart through the opening. Fill the heart until it is plump but not overstuffed. Fold the raw edges of the fabric to the inside, and hand stitch the opening closed.

sew on bows Make five small bows from the ribbon and sew by hand to the center top of each heart shape. Use doubled sewing thread to make sure the bows are securely attached.

sew hearts together With right sides together, securely whipstitch the hearts into a chain. To make sure the decoration is sturdy and secure, each row of stitches should be approximately ¾in (1.5cm) in length.

finishing Cut two lengths of cotton tape, each approximately 1yd. (1m) long, and fold in half. Securely hand stitch the center fold of one ribbon to each end of the row of fabric hearts. Tie to the bars of the crib.

hints and tips

• The crib decoration can also be made
in pretty vintage-style pastels for a little girl
• Try adding a little dried lavender wrapped in
cheesecloth to the center of the stuffing—
the fragrance is said to promote restful sleep.

button-trimmed frames

Even the simplest of frames can be
transformed by a coat of paint and some
decorative additions, such as a handful
of pretty mother-of-pearl buttons.

WHAT YOU WILL NEED
wooden picture frame • sandpaper,
if necessary • undercoat • non-toxic
paint • buttons for decoration • glue
• two or three paintbrushes • non-toxic
water-based acrylic varnish, if required

gather materials Decant small amounts of the paint into glass dishes. Make sure the glue is close at hand to apply the buttons.

apply undercoat If the wooden frame has any rough edges, sand it before applying the paint to provide a key. Next, apply a coat of undercoat. Let the undercoat dry thoroughly before applying the next coat of paint.

paint frame Paint the frame with the main color and let it dry thoroughly. A second coat of paint may be necessary to achieve perfect coverage. Leave the frame to dry. If preferred, finish with a coat of protective water-based acrylic varnish.

decorate frame Arrange the buttons around the frame to work out the correct spacings. Now apply a dab of glue to the back of each button and glue it to the frame. Leave to dry completely. Insert your chosen picture or photograph to finish.

sailing away

We painted this small frame in a cheery sky-blue shade and added white buttons at each corner. The picture was made from a scrap of fabric appliquéd to a square of blue gingham.

WHAT YOU WILL NEED

wooden picture frame • sandpaper, if necessary
• undercoat • non-toxic paint • two or three paintbrushes
• water-based non-toxic acrylic varnish, if required
• buttons to decorate • glue • scissors • gingham fabric
• small scrap of fabric printed with suitable image • thread

paint frame A light sanding with sandpaper will make the wood smooth for painting. Apply a coat of undercoat and let it dry thoroughly. Now apply a top coat of paint. A second coat may be required for good coverage. Let it dry completely. If desired, apply a coat of water-based acrylic varnish for a more durable finish.

decorate Apply glue to the back of the buttons and stick one in each corner of the frame. Let them dry. Cut a piece of gingham fabric slightly larger than the frame opening. Now cut a smaller piece of a different fabric and baste to the gingham. Machine stitch in place using a zigzag stitch and contrasting cotton thread.

pretty in pink

This pretty frame would be a perfect gift for a little girl's nursery. Painted in softest marshmallow pink, it is decorated with a selection of flower-shaped plastic buttons and frames a wooden letter painted the same delicate pink as the frame.

WHAT YOU WILL NEED

wooden picture frame • wooden letter • sandpaper, if necessary • undercoat • non-toxic paint • two or three paintbrushes • water-based non-toxic acrylic varnish, if required • buttons to decorate • glue

paint frame and letter Remove the glass and back from the frame. Sandpaper the frame and letter so they are smooth. Apply a coat of undercoat and let it dry. Now paint the frame and wooden letter. Apply a second coat of paint for good coverage and leave to dry. Apply a coat of water-based acrylic varnish for a durable finish, if necessary.

decorate Apply a dab of glue to the back of each button and arrange them all the way around the opening of the frame. Leave to dry. Glue the painted wooden letter to a sturdy piece of white mat board and insert it in the frame. Finally, fit the back of the frame in place.

painted wooden letters

These painted letters can be used to decorate
a wall, shelf, or mantelpiece. You could either opt
for baby's initials, or his or her first name.

WHAT YOU WILL NEED

undercoat • non-toxic paints in
two different shades • wooden letters
• fine paintbrushes • soft pencil
• ruler, if necessary • water-based
non-toxic acrylic varnish

apply undercoat Decant small amounts of the paint into glass dishes. If unpainted, apply undercoat to prime the letters for decoration. The more solid the undercoat, the easier it will be to apply the colored paint, so apply two coats if necessary to achieve good coverage.

apply base coat Apply one or two coats of your chosen background color to each wooden letter, allowing them to dry completely between coats. If you are using light colors, use the palest color as the base coat so it's easier to cover with the second color when you paint on the decorative details.

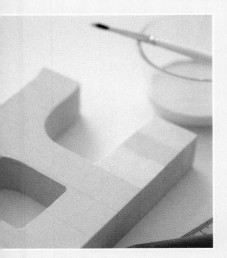

draw on design Use a soft pencil to draw the stripes (use a ruler, if necessary) or dots on the letters. Fill in the second color using a fine paintbrush. Fill in the edges of the design using a very fine brush first, then use a slightly thicker one to finish.

finishing You may need to apply a second coat for best results. If you smudge the paint or make any mistakes, use the base color and a fine paintbrush to rectify them. Once the letters have dried, apply a coat of acrylic varnish to seal the paint and give a hard-wearing finish.

trimmed baby blankets

Soft blankets in pastel tones are both a pretty and practical gift for a new baby. Here, simple embroidery and appliqué techniques have been used to customize purchased blankets.

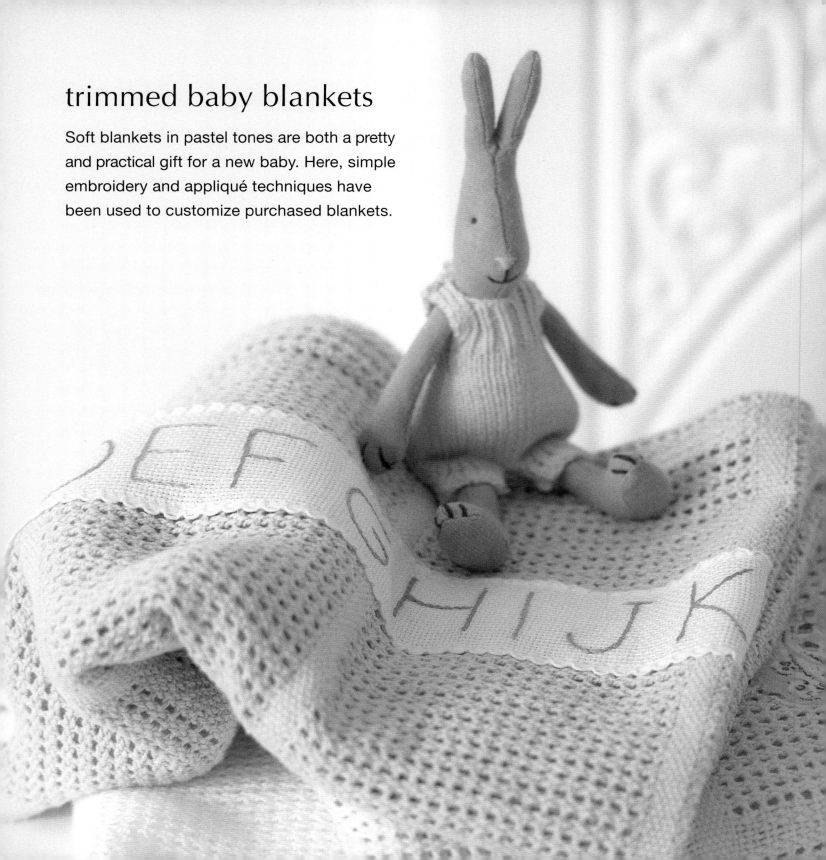

WHAT YOU WILL NEED

cotton baby blanket • 2in (5cm) wide Evenweave or Aida needlework band, to fit width of blanket, plus 1¼in (3cm) • fabric pen • selection of pastel embroidery thread • needle • thread • sewing machine

cut ribbon to fit Measure the width of the blanket and add 1¼in (3cm) to this measurement. Cut the needlework band to this size, all ready for embroidery.

draw the letters Use a fabric pen to draw the letters of the alphabet along the needlework band. You could print the letters from a computer and trace them, if preferred. Try decorative typefaces for a different effect.

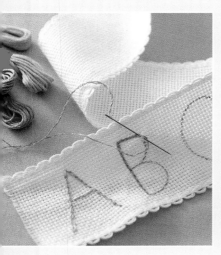

embroider letters Using two strands of embroidery floss, work the letters in tiny chain stitch (see Techniques, page 115). We used a selection of different pastel colors and alternated them for variety.

finishing When the embroidery is complete, place the band on the blanket 4in (10cm) from the top edge, and baste in place. Fold under the raw edges of the band to stop them fraying, then fold them to the back of the blanket. To finish, use a sewing machine to topstitch in place.

appliquéd hearts

Perfect for a little girl, this cozy pink baby blanket has been decorated with a row of hearts snipped from left-over vintage floral fabric in a coordinating color. The edges of the blanket are bound in pink bias binding to match.

WHAT YOU WILL NEED

scissors • pastel-colored cotton baby blanket • piece of bias binding equal in length to all four edges of the blanket • sewing thread • sewing machine • scraps of pretty, vintage-style fabric • fusible web • matching thread for appliqué

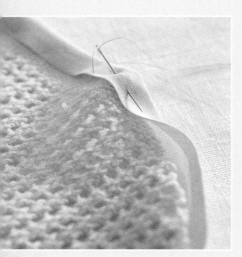

edge blanket Cut the hem off the top and bottom of the blanket and round off the corners. Fold a ⅛in (3mm) hem down each side of the the bias binding and press. Fold the bias binding in half, so the folded edges meet, and press. Place it around the blanket, sandwiching the raw edges, and baste. Using a machine, topstitch in place.

add hearts Iron fusible web to the back of the floral fabric and cut out five heart shapes. Peel off the backing paper and iron the hearts close to the top edge of the blanket, spacing them evenly. Using a sewing machine, zigzag stitch around the edges two or three times, so that any raw edges are concealed.

pastel squares

Simple straight stitch in three pastel colors is used to decorate the edges of this cellular blanket, using the holes in the blanket knit as a guide.

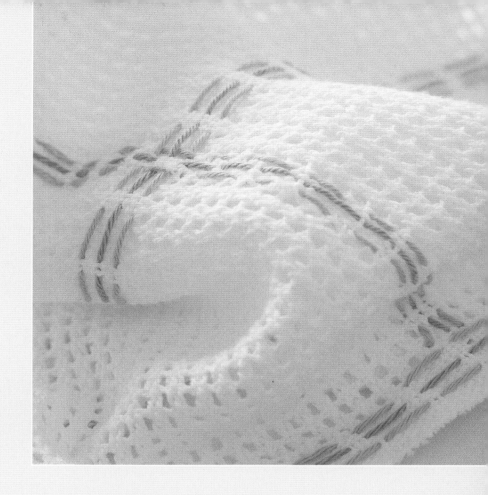

WHAT YOU WILL NEED
needle • pearl cotton embroidery thread in three different pastel shades • pastel-colored cellular blanket

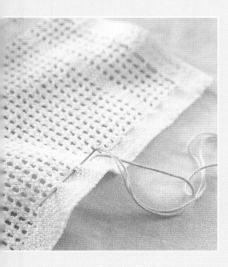

make first line of stitching Thread the needle with the first color and stitch along the bottom edge of the blanket. The stitches should be approximately ⅛in (3mm) apart. Work them all around the edges of the blanket. Now begin stitching with the next color just above the first. When you have finished, repeat the process with the final color.

finishing The inner stitching is worked in the same way, starting approximately ½in (1cm) from the edge of the blanket. Following the squares of the blanket as a guide, use the same colors of embroidery thread to repeat the rows of stitches all the way up and across the blanket.

appliquéd
laundry bag

This cute and practical laundry
bag is decorated with baby clothing
motifs appliquéd to the bag using
zigzag stitch and trimmed with tiny
buttons and bows.

WHAT YOU WILL NEED

20 x 32in (50 x 80cm) white fabric
• 1yd. (1m) ribbon, ¾in (1.5cm) wide
• pins • needle • thread • sewing
machine • paper • pencil • scissors
• fabrics for appliqué • fusible web
• thread for appliqué • two ribbon bows
• button • 1yd. (1m) needlework band
• 2½yds. (2.2m) piping cord

pin ribbon border Lay the cotton fabric flat. Lay the gingham ribbon along the bottom of the longest edge of the fabric, approximately 3in (7cm) from the bottom of the fabric. Pin in place, then baste to the fabric by hand.

stitch border in place Using a sewing machine, sew the ribbon border to the fabric using a narrow zigzag stitch so the stitches just enclose the ribbon. Now press the fabric on the wrong side to flatten the stitching.

cut out appliqué motifs Trace the templates on page 119 onto paper and cut them out. Iron fusible web to the back of the fabric scraps. Draw around the templates on the paper side of the fusible web and cut out. Peel off the backing paper and position the motifs, right side up, on the bag above the ribbon border. Iron in place with a hot iron.

stitch around motifs Using a machine, stitch around the motifs using zigzag stitch in matching thread. Use a loose stitch and repeat the stitching two or three times to cover any raw edges. Several rows of stitching are better than one tight row, which can cause the fabric to pucker.

decorate motifs Press the wrong side of the fabric to flatten the zigzag stitching. Stitch one small ribbon bow to the center of the skirt motif and the other to the top of the trouser motif. Sew the button to the front of the T-shirt motif.

cut needlework band Cut two lengths of needlework band measuring 16½in (42cm) each. Fold the ends ½in (1cm) to the inside and pin. Hand stitch these edges in place, then press. Set aside. Now fold the bag fabric in half, with wrong sides together. Make sure that the edges of the gingham ribbon line up. Pin in place and baste around the edges, leaving the top edge open, to form a bag. Stitch the edges using a sewing machine. Trim and clip the corners. Now fold down a 2in (5cm) hem from the top edge of the bag and press.

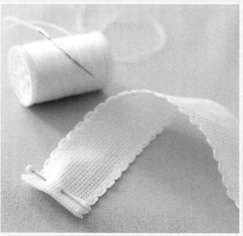

attach band Lay the first piece of needlework band along the top edge of one side of the bag, covering the raw edges of the hem. Pin, baste, and topstitch in place along the top and bottom of the band. Repeat on the other side of the bag with the second piece of band. Make sure the open ends of the band line up at the sides of the bag.

finishing Cut two 1¼yds. (1.1m) lengths of piping cord. Bind the ends of the cord with tape, then insert a safety pin. Push the cord into one open end of the band and feed through. Knot the ends. Use the safety pin on the second piece of cord and insert it in the opposite opening. Thread through, knot the ends and pull the drawstring ties to finish.

hints and tips

• You can opt for different fabrics depending on the baby's sex—blue polka dots were used for this slightly more boyish version.

• Adjust the size of the bag to make a washbag. Cut a piece of fabric 12 x 20in (30 x 50cm) and use a photocopier to reduce the motifs.

decorated hangers

Plain wooden hangers are available from most
department stores and can be painted to match a nursery
scheme. We used pastel tones decorated with tiny polka
dots and finished with coordinating gingham ribbon.

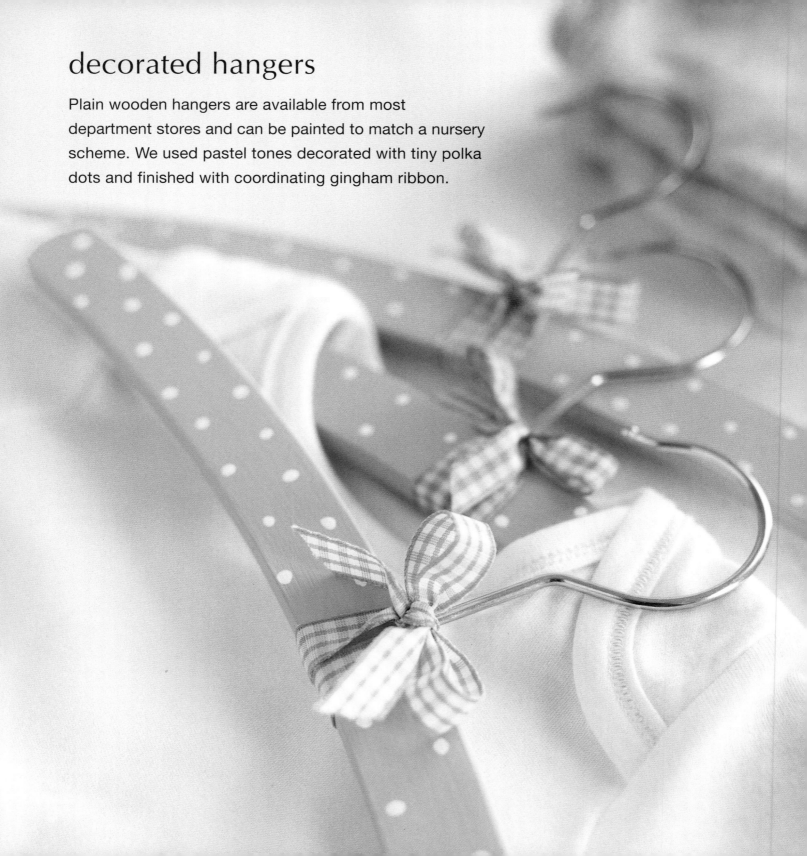

WHAT YOU WILL NEED

plain wooden hangers • sandpaper, if necessary • masking tape • fine paintbrushes • undercoat • non-toxic paints in two or three different shades • non-toxic white paint • non-toxic water-based acrylic varnish • ¼yd. 25cm gingham ribbon per hanger

prepare hangers If there are any rough edges on the hanger, sand them down. Cut a piece of masking tape and wind it around the metal arm of the hanger to prevent paint from running onto it. Apply a coat of undercoat and leave to dry. Apply a further coat, if required.

apply base color When the undercoat is completely dry, apply the base color to the hanger using a fine paintbrush. Let it dry thoroughly before applying a second coat for good, even coverage.

decorate Use a very fine paintbrush to decorate the hanger with tiny white dots. We spaced the dots about ½in (1cm) apart. Paint them on one side of the hanger and leave to dry. Repeat on the other side. When dry, apply a coat of acrylic varnish to finish.

finishing Cut a length of gingham ribbon ¼yd (25cm) long. Fold it in half and loop the center around the top of the hanger. Tie the ends in a bow and trim with scissors. Cut the ends on the diagonal to prevent them from fraying.

lined storage baskets

Baskets are a great addition to any nursery,
providing easily accessible storage for everything
from toys to diapers. Make them pretty as well as
practical by lining them with fabrics that
match the nursery
scheme.

WHAT YOU WILL NEED
basket • pencil • scissors • printed
cotton fabric, 44in (137cm) wide
• sewing machine • cotton ribbon,
approx ½in (1cm) wide • safety pin

create a template Use your basket
as a template. Place it on the fabric and
draw around the base, adding ¾in (1.5cm)
seam allowance all around. Measure the
depth of the basket, adding ¾in (1.5cm)
seam allowance. Add another 6in (15cm) to
the depth of the lining for the folded edge.

cut out and stitch lining Cut out two pieces of fabric. You
will have one smaller rectangle for the base and a long wide strip for
the sides of the basket. Zigzag all around the edges to prevent the
pieces of fabric from fraying. Fold the long strip of fabric in half, right
sides together, so the two shorter edges meet. Pin, then baste a
seam in place, then machine stitch the edges together. Press the
seam open using a hot iron.

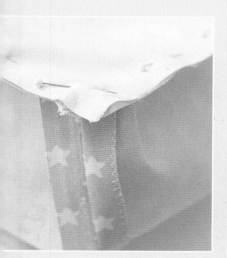

stitch base to lining With right side down, pin the base of the basket lining to the
main section, making sure that one corner of the base lines up neatly with the side seam.
You may need to notch the corners of the base section to make it easier to stitch. Baste
the edges and machine stitch together.

trim and clip corners Using sharp
scissors, trim and clip the seams so that
they lie flat. Press using a hot iron.

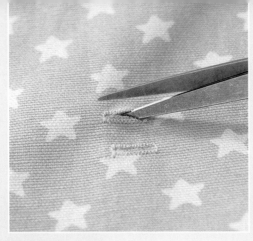

make openings Fit the lining into the basket and fold it out over the top edge of the basket so you can see where you want to put the openings for the ribbon ties. Mark two openings ½in (1cm) apart, then work them using the buttonhole setting on a sewing machine. Slit open with scissors.

stitch casing Fold down a 1½in (4cm) hem from the top edge of the lining fabric and press flat. Pin, then baste in place. Now, using a sewing machine, topstitch all around the lining 1½in (4cm) down from the top to create the casing for the ribbon drawstrings.

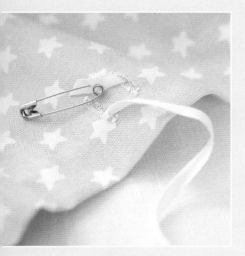

insert ribbon ties Measure the circumference of the basket lining and add 20in (50cm). Cut a length of ribbon to fit this measurement, and anchor a safety pin to the end. Insert the ribbon into the casing through one opening. Work the ribbon all the way through the casing and out of the second one. Remove the safety pin from the end of the ribbon.

finishing Fit the lining over the basket, folding approximately 4in (10cm) over the top edge of the basket. Tighten the ribbons and tie in a bow. To prevent the ends of the ribbon from fraying, trim them diagonally.

hints and tips

For a pretty yet coordinated effect, use differently patterned fabrics
in the same color to line a row of baskets for a nursery shelf.

funky flowers crib mobile

These funky three-dimensional flowers are cut from simple felt squares and decorated with flower-shaped buttons. The mobile will make a fun and fascinating addition to any crib.

WHAT YOU WILL NEED

paper for template • pencil • scissors • pins • four 8in (20cm) squares of felt per flower (two squares each of two different colors) • sewing machine • thread • synthetic-fiber filling • needle • button • 5yds. (4m) white tape, approx $\frac{1}{4}$in (6mm) wide • metal hoop, approx 12in (30cm) diameter • glue

make templates Trace the two flower templates on page 117 onto plain paper and cut them out. Each flower is made up of two larger flower shapes, which we cut from bright pink felt, and two smaller flowers, which we cut from pale pink felt. Pin the templates to the fabric and cut out.

stitch flowers Stitch the flower shapes together using the zigzag stitch on a sewing machine. You may need to work one or two extra rows of zigzag stitches around the edges to cover. It is better to use a slightly looser stitch and repeat it several times, as a very close stitch tends to pucker the fabric.

cut opening and fill flower Using sharp scissors, snip a small opening about $\frac{3}{4}$in (1.5cm) long in the center of one side of the flower (make sure you do not cut through both layers). Use a pencil to push the stuffing into the flower shape. The flower should be plump but not overstuffed. Stitch the opening closed by hand.

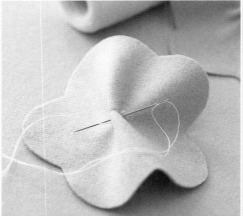

pleat flowers Pinch a pleat in the center of the smaller outer flower and work a few stitches by hand to hold it in place. This gives the outer flowers their three-dimensional effect. Repeat on the other outer flower.

assemble flowers Sandwich the stuffed flower between the two smaller flowers. Push the needle through all the layers to attach the smaller flowers. Make several sturdy stitches to hold the smaller flowers firmly in place.

sew on buttons Place a button in the center of the smaller flower and stitch through all the layers to secure it in place. Stitch another button to the center of the corresponding flower on the other side.

attach cotton tape Cut a length of cotton tape approximately 4in (10cm) long for each flower. Fold one end ¼in (5mm) to the inside and neatly hand stitch to the curved edge of the central stuffed flower.

finishing Wrap the cotton tape around the hoop so all the metal is covered. Hold the tape in a small bundle as you wrap, to prevent it from tangling. Apply glue or double-sided tape every 2in (5cm), to hold the tape in place. When it is dry, mark positions for the flowers on the hoop and stitch each one in place by hand.

hints and tips

• These soft, plump stars cut from blue felt and finished with a star-shaped button are perfect for a boy's nursery. A star-shaped template can be found on page 117.

• Metal hoops can be obtained from florist's shops, although the circular frame of an old lampshade would be a good alternative.

decorated lampshades

Inexpensive purchased lampshades can easily be customized to make a pretty and unusual gift for the nursery. Paint the base to match, and decorate with a simple design.

WHAT YOU WILL NEED

wooden lamp base • two paintbrushes • undercoat • non-toxic paint in two colors • soft white pencil • non-toxic water-based acrylic varnish • plain fabric lampshade • 2yds. (2m) narrow silk ribbon • needle • thread • scissors • thimble, if necessary • 12 flower-shaped buttons

apply undercoat If the wood is bare, you will have to apply an undercoat to prime the lamp base for decoration. If necessary, apply two coats to achieve good coverage. Let it dry. Now paint the lamp base in your chosen color.

decorate the lampbase Use a soft white pencil to draw a scallop design on the base of the lamp. Fill in with paint, using a very fine paintbrush, and let it dry. Apply a second coat to finish. Apply a coat of water-based acrylic varnish to seal the paint, and leave it to dry thoroughly.

sew on bows Make twelve ribbon bows from the silk ribbon and cut the ends on the diagonal to prevent them from fraying. Hand sew the first bow onto the lampshade about ¾in (1.5cm) up from the base of the shade. Sew on the remaining bows, making sure they are evenly spaced. If the lampshade is stiff, you may need to use a thimble.

finishing Sew a flower-shaped mother-of-pearl button by hand to the center of each bow to finish. Again, it is advisable to use a thimble while sewing if the lampshade is particularly stiff.

buttoned up

White buttons make a decorative addition to this blue waffle fabric lampshade. We used matching embroidery thread to sew on the buttons, so that the stitching also becomes a decorative feature.

WHAT YOU WILL NEED

waffle or other fabric lampshade • pen • 24 small buttons in an attractive color or shape • embroidery thread • scissors • thimble, if necessary

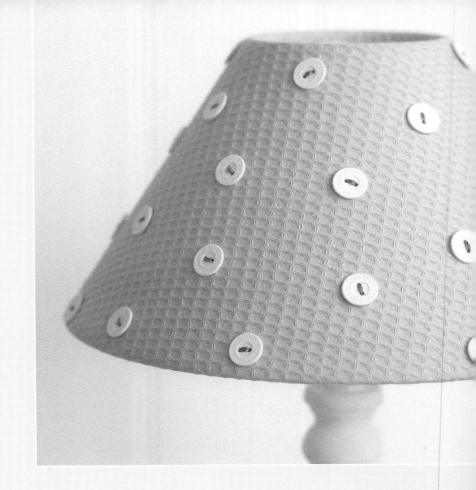

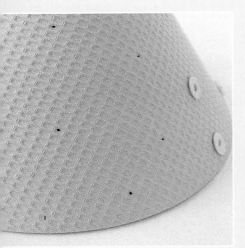

mark button positions Use a pen to mark the position of the buttons on the lampshade before sewing. We spaced them approximately 1½in (4cm) apart. Alternatively, you could attach them in a row along the bottom edge of the shade.

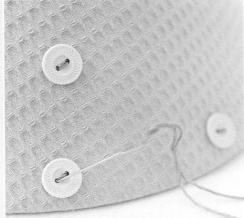

sew on buttons Sew through the center of the button using embroidery thread. You may wish to use a thimble if the shade is particularly stiff. Repeat for the rest of the buttons until the lampshade is finished.

rickrack trim

Three rows of bold blue rickrack liven up a white lampshade. The lamp base was painted a gentle sky blue to pick up the color of the trim.

WHAT YOU WILL NEED

wooden lamp base • two paintbrushes • undercoat (if lamp base is unpainted) • non-toxic paint in two colors • non-toxic water-based acrylic varnish • plain fabric lampshade • rickrack • scissors • glue

paint lamp base If the lamp base is bare wood, you will have to apply an undercoat to prime it for decoration. If necessary, apply two coats to achieve good coverage. Let it dry. Now paint the lamp base in your chosen color. Apply a second coat to finish, followed by a coat of water-based acrylic varnish to seal the paint. Let it dry.

attach trim Measure the circumference of the lampshade to decide how long each piece of rickrack should be. Add ¾in (1.5cm) to each measurement. Cut three lengths of braid and glue to the shade in three rows spaced an equal distance apart. Fold the raw ends of the rickrack under and apply more glue to secure in place.

painted building blocks

Wooden blocks make a decorative addition to any nursery,
but that's not all—as baby grows up into an active toddler, he
or she will have hours of fun building up and knocking down
these chunky blocks. To decorate the blocks, we used
a variety of bold, simple stencils.

WHAT YOU WILL NEED

plain wooden blocks • sandpaper, if necessary • undercoat • non-toxic paints in a variety of different shades • stencils of your choice • masking tape • soft pencil • scissors • fine paintbrushes • ruler • water-based non-toxic acrylic varnish

gather materials Decant small amounts of the paint into glass dishes. Have a flat plate on hand to hold the stenciling paint.

apply undercoat Lightly sand the blocks with sandpaper to smooth edges if necessary. Apply undercoat to prime the letters for decoration. The more solid the undercoat, the easier it will be to apply the colored paint, so apply two coats if necessary to achieve good coverage. Paint the top and sides first, and let them dry before painting the bottom of the cube.

paint blocks Paint the blocks in an array of different colors and let them dry completely. Apply a further coat of paint to each to provide smooth, complete coverage.

stencil motifs Place a stencil on one side of the block and use masking tape to hold it in place. Load your brush with paint, then blot it. Dab on the paint. Let it dry and stencil another coat if required. Let it dry, remove the stencil and repeat the process on the other sides of the block. When dry, varnish the finished block.

hearts and flowers

Simple stenciled hearts and hand-painted flowers decorate these gorgeous wooden blocks in shades of soft green, pink, and white. Almost too pretty to play with, they would be a decorative addition to a shelf or mantelpiece in a little girl's nursery.

WHAT YOU WILL NEED

plain wooden blocks • non-toxic paints in a variety of colors • masking tape • stencils of your choice • soft pencil • scissors • fine paintbrushes • water-based non-toxic acrylic varnish

stencil blocks Paint the sides of each block in alternate colors (we used pink, white, and soft green). Let them dry between each coat. It may help to use masking tape around the edges of each block to prevent the paint from running. When the block has been painted and is dry, use masking tape to hold your first stencil in place and fill in with paint.

draw other shapes If you can't find stencils you like, try drawing shapes freehand. Here, we drew flower shapes using a soft pencil. Fill in the petals and centers with different-colored paints and let them dry thoroughly. Finally, add a coat of acrylic varnish for a hard-wearing finish.

big bold numbers

These fun blocks are decorated with a simple design of stenciled numerals. Not only are they great fun to build up and knock down, but they make learning numbers easy, too!

WHAT YOU WILL NEED
plain wooden blocks • non-toxic paints in a variety of colors • masking tape • stencils of your choice • fine paintbrushes • water-based non-toxic acrylic varnish

paint blocks Paint the sides of each block in alternating colors (we used blue and white). Let them dry between each coat. It may be helpful to use masking tape around the edges of each block to stop the paint from running.

stencil blocks When the block is dry, use masking tape to hold your first stencil in place. Stencil the design, making sure you remove as much paint as possible from the brush. Let it dry, then apply another coat of paint. When dry, remove the masking tape and stencil. Repeat on the other sides. When dry, varnish the finished block.

KEEPSAKES

pretty patchwork blanket

This blanket is made of the softest pink and blue wool squares and embroidered with motifs worked in chain stitch using yarn. It makes a wonderful keepsake and could also be used as a wallhanging.

WHAT YOU WILL NEED

paper for templates • pencil • scissors • 20in (50cm) pale pink fine wool fabric • 20in (50cm) pale blue fine wool fabric • fabric marker pen • needle • tapestry yarn • sewing thread • 1yd (1m) cotton fabric for backing the blanket • pins • sewing machine

cut fabric squares and templates

Trace the various templates on page 120 onto a piece of paper and cut them out. Now cut six blue wool squares and six pink wool squares, each one measuring 10 x 10in (24 x 24cm).

draw motifs Place the squares on a table to plan where each motif should be drawn and on what color square. Place a template in the center of each square and draw around it using the fabric marker pen. Draw in any details such as eyes and other markings by hand. Draw one motif on each of the 12 fabric squares, making sure there is a variety of different motifs, so adjacent squares will not feature the same one.

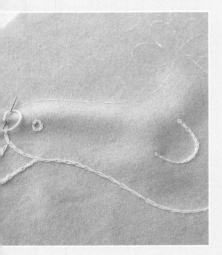

embroider Using a single skein of tapestry yarn, begin working chain stitch over the marked motifs (see Techniques, page 115). Work eyes in French knots (see Techniques, page 114). Embroider all 12 squares and press flat on the back of the fabric.

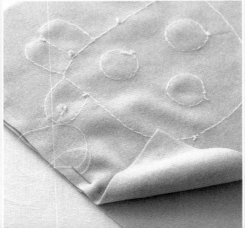

stitch squares With right sides together, and alternating between blue and pink squares, stitch the squares together with ½in (1cm) seams. Use three squares for each row of the quilt. When you have made four rows, stitch them together with a ½in (1cm) seam to form the finished quilt.

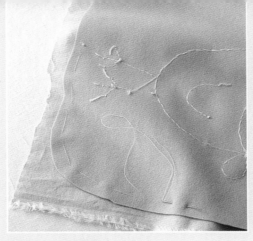

baste quilt to lining Press the seams flat. With right sides together, lay the quilt on the lining fabric and pin them together. Cut a curve on each corner of the quilt, then baste the quilt to the lining, leaving an opening of 6in (15cm) along one edge, for turning the quilt right side out.

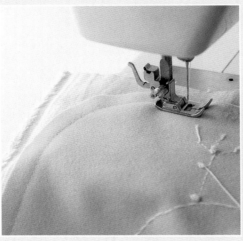

machine stitch Stitch around all edges of the quilt and lining fabric using a sewing machine, leaving the 6in (15cm) opening to allow for turning the quilt right side out. When you have finished, press the quilt on the backing.

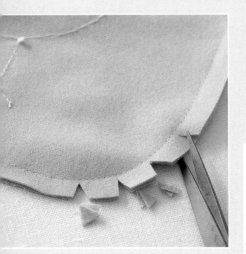

cut and clip Use a sharp pair of scissors to trim and clip the curved corners of the quilt so it lies flat when turned right side out. Clip as close to the stitching as possible without actually cutting the stitches. Turn the quilt right side out and press flat.

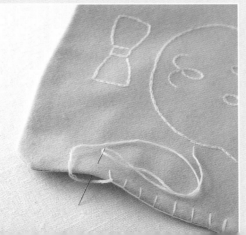

finishing Using small whipstitch, hand sew the opening of the quilt closed. Using tapestry yarn, work blanket stitch approximately ½in (1cm) apart all the way around the edges of the quilt (see Techniques, page 112).

hints and tips

To make the quilt into a wallhanging, simply stitch a length of Aida or Evenweave needlework band to the back of the quilt at the top edge, leaving the two ends of the tape open. Insert a length of narrow wooden dowel and attach a length of ribbon (in a pretty coordinating color) to each end of the dowel. Now hang the quilt from the ribbon.

painted chair

A child's painted chair is a very special
gift, not least because it is likely to become
a family heirloom. Look for cute vintage
chairs in flea markets or at garage sales.
Alternatively, department and furniture stores
stock child-sized wooden chairs that can
be customized for a personal touch.

WHAT YOU WILL NEED

child's wooden chair • sandpaper, if necessary • undercoat • non-toxic paints in two colors • fine and medium-sized paintbrushes • stencils of your choice • masking tape • water-based non-toxic acrylic varnish

prepare chair If the chair has any rough edges, sand them down ready for painting (if it's a secondhand chair, you may need to strip the existing paint). Apply one or two coats of undercoat and let them dry completely between each coat.

apply paint Paint the chair in the main color using a medium-sized paintbrush. It is best to paint the front and sides first, then let them dry before turning it upside down so you can reach the insides of the legs and underneath the seat. You may need to apply a second coat for smooth, even coverage.

stencil design Position the stencil on the seat. Hold it in place with small pieces of masking tape. Apply the paint to the stencil, using a stencil brush. Make sure you remove as much paint from the brush as possible before stenciling, so the paint does not bleed. Let it dry and apply a further coat of paint if necessary.

remove stencil When the paint is dry, carefully remove the masking tape and peel off the stencil. Finish the chair with one or two coats of water-based acrylic varnish and let it dry thoroughly.

cozy cushion

After painting a wooden chair a
pretty shade of soft lilac, we softened
it up with the addition of a cute padded
cushion tied on with ribbon bows.

WHAT YOU WILL NEED

paper for template • pencil • scissors • cotton fabric
in a shade to match the chair • pins • sewing machine
• polyester batting • 20in (50cm) gingham ribbon

make cushion Draw around the chair seat on a piece of paper to make a template.
Add ¾in (1.5cm) seam allowances all around. Pin the template to the fabric and cut out
two pieces. Place them right sides together, and pin, then machine stitch, leaving the back
edge open. Clip the curved edges and turn right side out. Cut a piece of batting using
the paper template, and trim ¾in (1.5cm) all around. Insert into the fabric pocket.

finishing Cut two 10in (25cm) lengths of
ribbon. Fold each piece in half. Insert the
folded edge of one ribbon into one corner
of the back section. Hand stitch in place.
Insert the other ribbon at the other corner
and stitch in place, then sew the opening
of the cushion closed. Trim the ribbon
ends diagonally to prevent fraying.

candy stripes

Two shades of pink have been used to decorate the slatted seat and bars of this chair. This would look equally cute in shades of blue for a baby boy.

WHAT YOU WILL NEED

child's wooden chair • sandpaper, if necessary • undercoat • non-toxic paints in two shades of pink • medium-sized paintbrushes • water-based non-toxic acrylic varnish

prepare chair If the chair has any rough edges, sand them down ready for painting (if it's a secondhand chair, you may need to strip the existing paint). Apply one or two coats of undercoat and let them dry completely between each coat. Now apply the paler pink shade to the whole chair, leaving alternate seat slats and back bars unpainted.

fill in stripes Paint the alternate slats and back bars in the darker shade of pink paint and let them dry. Apply a further coat. When dry, finish the chair with one or two coats of water-based acrylic varnish.

stenciled toybox

Transform an old blanket chest by reinventing it as a toybox. This one was painted, then stenciled with a row of cheery little ducks. Look out for boxes or trunks in secondhand stores. Alternatively, buy a plain toybox and customize it for a special new arrival!

WHAT YOU WILL NEED

wooden toybox • sandpaper, if necessary • undercoat • non-toxic paints in two colors • fine and medium-sized paintbrushes • stencils of your choice • masking tape • water-based non-toxic acrylic varnish

paint stripe Sand and undercoat the toybox. When dry, use masking tape to mark out the stripe around the bottom of the box. Smooth the masking tape to make sure the paint cannot bleed at the edges. Apply a coat of paint. When dry, apply a second coat and let dry.

position first stencil Using a pencil, mark out the positions of the stencils, evenly spacing them along the front of the toybox. Place the stencil in the first position, using masking tape to fix it securely in place. Using a stencil brush, apply a coat of paint, first making sure you remove as much paint from the brush as possible, to stop the paint from bleeding under the edges of the stencil. Let it dry, then apply a further coat if necessary.

repeat stencil motif Lift the stencil from the box and fix it in the next position, using masking tape. Apply paint with the stencil brush, and let it dry thoroughly. Add a second coat, if necessary. Continue to stencil all the way along the front of the box and onto both sides. We also added a single duck motif to the lid of the box.

remove masking tape When the stenciling is complete and all the paint has dried, remove the masking tape from the painted stripe. To personalize the toybox further, you could add baby's name or initials and date of birth, either using stencils or painting freehand.

hand-embroidered pillow

This beautiful pillow is decorated with silk ribbon embroidery and ribbon rosettes, with baby's name worked in tiny chain stitch. Instead of a pillow form, you could fill it with dried lavender wrapped in cheesecloth— the scent is said to aid restful sleep.

WHAT YOU WILL NEED

paper for templates • pencil • black pen • scissors • two 16in (40cm) squares of linen fabric • pins • fabric pen • green and pink embroidery floss • needle • silk ribbon in four colors • six ribbon rosettes • sewing machine • 6in (15cm) gingham ribbon, ½in (1cm) wide • pillow form

create templates Trace the templates for the front and back of the hearts on page 121 onto a piece of paper. Use a black pen to draw the embroidery motif onto the heart-shaped template, making sure the outline is dark enough to see through the fabric.

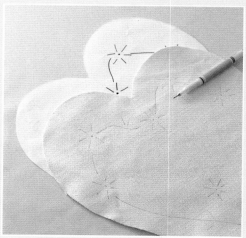

cut out fabric Pin the templates to the linen fabric and cut out one heart shape and two back sections with seam allowance. Lay the heart shape on top of the paper template and carefully trace over the design using a fabric pen. Write the baby's name freehand in the center of the heart (you may wish to use different lettering).

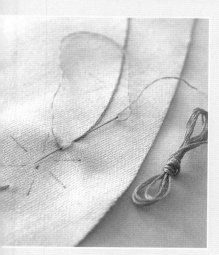

embroider stems Using green embroidery thread, work the stems of the flowers in chain stitch (see Techniques, page 115). Now use green silk ribbon to chain stitch the leaves. Make sure the ribbon is as flat as possible as you pull it through the fabric. Press the embroidery flat on the reverse of the fabric.

work ribbon flowers Use pale pink, mauve and pink silk ribbon to embroider the flowers using single chain stitch. Keep the ribbon as flat as possible as you pull it through the fabric. Work two mauve, two pale pink, and two darker pink flowers. Press the fabric from the wrong side.

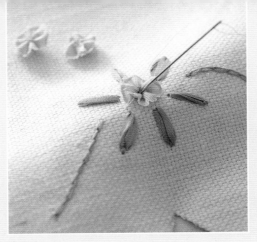

attach ribbon rosettes Stitch a ribbon rosette to the center of each silk ribbon flower. Use several stitches to make sure the rosette is firmly secured.

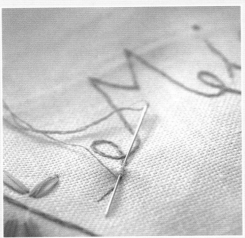

embroider baby's name Use small chain stitch (see Techniques, page 115) to work the baby's name in the center of the cushion. If you prefer (or if the name is too long to fit), the name can be omitted or replaced with another ribbon flower.

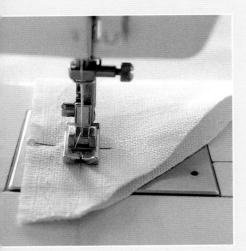

sew back section Place the two back sections of the pillow cover right sides together. Pin along the straight edge, leaving an opening that starts 2in (5cm) from the bottom and ¾in (1.5cm) from the top. Using a sewing machine, stitch from the bottom of the cover to the pin, then repeat at the top. Trim the corners, then press the seam open.

finishing Place the pillow cover right sides together. Using a sewing machine, stitch the front and back sections together. Trim and clip the curved edges, turn right side out, and press. Insert the pillow form. Make a loop of gingham ribbon and stitch it just inside the back opening. Finally, whipstitch the opening closed.

hints and tips

• Use floral fabric and work the embroidered ribbon flowers over the printed designs for a 3D effect.

• If you don't enjoy hand sewing, make a cushion from fabric that's already been embroidered. Look out for pretty vintage embroidered tablecloths or tray cloths in thrift stores or at rummage sales.

photo album

Welcome a new baby with this gorgeous personalized photo album, made using iron-on printed paper and decorated with delicate mother-of-pearl buttons.

WHAT YOU WILL NEED

photo or preferred image • one sheet
iron-on transfer paper • photo album
• enough linen fabric 44in (137cm)
wide to cover the album • 30 buttons,
to decorate • needle • 16in (40cm)
narrow silk ribbon • masking tape
• paper for lining • strong glue

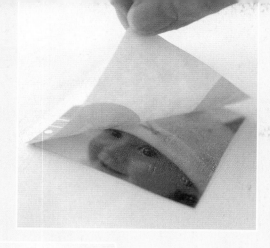

apply iron-on transfer Following the
manufacturer's instructions, photocopy
your chosen image on the iron-on transfer
paper. Cut out the image and iron it to the
linen fabric, positioning it so it will end up
at the center front of the album. Let it cool.
Peel off the backing paper.

sew on buttons We used alternating mother-of-pearl buttons in
flower, star, and square shapes for the border. Arrange the buttons
around the image. Stitch each one on by hand. Thread four buttons
onto the length of silk ribbon to make a page marker, and knot at
the bottom to prevent them from coming off.

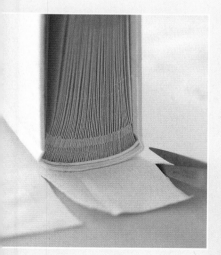

cut fabric Stand the album on its spine and open the back and front covers. Mark 1¼in
(3cm) around all edges and cut the fabric to this size. Cut two slits in the fabric from the
top edge of the fabric down to the spine. Repeat at the bottom of the album.

fold in spine Open the book wide so
that the inside of the spine is revealed and
apply a dab of glue to this area. Fold the
slit section of fabric inside and press firmly
in place until glue is dry. Insert the buttoned
length of ribbon inside the spine at the top
of the book, and glue in place.

make corners Working at the top of the album, neatly fold the edges of the fabric beside the spine section and glue in place. Repeat at the bottom of the album and let it dry completely.

glue edges Stand the album on its spine and open out the front cover. Working at the top of the album, apply glue to the underside of the fabric, then fold it neatly over the edge of the album to the inside. Press firmly in place. Use masking tape to hold the fabric neatly in place while the glue dries. Repeat this process on the back cover of the book.

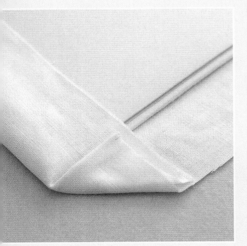

fold corners To finish the bottom corners of the album, fold up the fabric to create a neat corner, applying a dab of glue between each layer of fabric to keep it in place. Fold the remaining edge over and apply glue to this corner and along the edge of the book to fix the fabric to the book.

finishing Measure the inside of the album's covers and cut two pieces of decorative paper approximately ½in (1cm) smaller around all edges to line the covers and conceal the raw fabric edges. Apply glue to the wrong side of the paper and press firmly to the inside covers. Leave the album open until the glue has dried completely.

hints and tips

• Rather than using a photograph, you could spell out baby's name in buttons on the front of the album
• Alternatively, embroider baby's name on the piece of linen in chain stitch, and frame it with decorative buttons.

cross-stitch picture

Checked gingham fabric makes an ideal grid for easy cross stitch. Here it's been used as the basis for a cute house design. Add baby's name and date of birth for a special finishing touch.

WHAT YOU WILL NEED

tracing paper for template • pencil
• rectangular piece of gingham fabric
approx 13 x 9in (32 x 23cm)
• medium-weight iron-on interfacing
approx 13 x 9in (32 x 23cm) • red and
blue embroidery thread • needle
• wooden photo frame

create a template Cut a house-shaped template from tracing paper. Mark the door and windows. Iron the interfacing to the wrong side of the gingham and let it cool. Place the template on the right side of the fabric and use a pencil to mark the details with small dots.

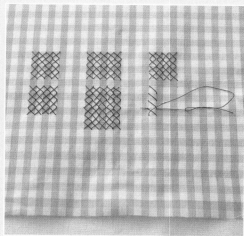

embroider door and windows Use two strands of red embroidery floss to work the door and five windows in cross stitch (see Techniques, page 113). Work four cross stitches in red embroidery thread for the two chimneys. Press on the wrong side.

embroider house Begin embroidering the main house in blue thread. Work in rows from the bottom up. To keep it flat, it is a good idea to iron out the cross stitch on the wrong side of the fabric at regular intervals during embroidery.

finishing Place the embroidery right side down and put the backing board of the photo frame on top. Fold one edge of fabric to the inside and push a needle through the fabric. Stitch across the backing board, pulling tight to stretch the embroidery. Fold in the other sides and stitch in place. Place in the frame to finish.

celebration plate

A simple plate decorated with baby's name and footprint celebrates baby's safe arrival and makes a wonderful keepsake. Most "paint-your-own" pottery shops will allow you take a plate home to work on, then return it to them for firing.

WHAT YOU WILL NEED
ceramic paints • unglazed plate • soft
brush • pencil • very fine paintbrush

paint baby's feet Apply a coat of
paint to the baby's feet using a soft brush.
It's a good idea to have a few test runs on
paper before working on the plate itself.
Press baby's foot firmly and gently down
on the plate, then remove so the paint
does not smudge. Let it dry.

draw design Use a fine pencil to draw a decorative design running
all around the border of the plate. You could incorporate the baby's
date of birth, if desired.

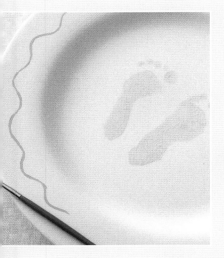

apply paint Use a very fine paintbrush to paint over the pencil design. Let the paint dry
completely. You may wish to apply a second coat if the paint color is very pale.

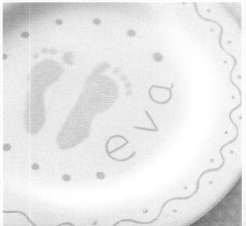

finishing Use the pencil to write baby's
name in the middle section of the plate. Use
a fine paintbrush to fill in these areas and
leave to dry. When complete, the plate can
be glazed and fired to finish.

PERFECT PRESENTATION

wrapped gifts

Beautiful gifts deserve beautiful presentation. And, by wrapping your gift imaginatively, you will add to the pleasure your friends or family experience on receiving it. The ideas for giftwrapping and cards on the following pages demonstrate that a gift is even more special when it's perfectly presented, especially if the wrapping is color-coordinated or hints at decorative elements that feature in the gift itself.

buttons and bows Beautiful presentation doesn't demand expensive gift wrap. This present was wrapped in plain white photocopy paper, then dressed up with a scrap of delicate lace wrapped around it and secured at the back. Another layer was added in the shape of a narrow, pale blue ribbon bow. The finishing touch is the tiny gift tag (a small price tag from a stationery shop) adorned with a delicate mother-of–pearl button.

boxing clever Awkwardly shaped gifts are difficult to tackle and can end up looking bulky, bulging, and messy. The solution is to use ready-made boxes to package awkward shapes. This simple cylindrical box (left) has been decorated with two layers of ribbon – a band of sheer organza topped with a band of gingham ribbon. Three fabric flowers were glued along the ribbon, and the box was finished with a miniature gift tag attached with a loop of narrow ribbon.

a hint of drama

Give a small gift an opulent feel by dressing it up with an oversized ribbon. Here (right), a small square box was wrapped in pearlized paper, then tied with a flamboyant organza ribbon bow. Narrow ribbon braid was threaded through and secured on the bottom of the box. To finish, a small gift tag in a harmonizing shade of blue was tied on with narrow satin ribbon.

creating texture

Layering paper, ribbon, and other elements make a gift feel extra-special. Here (above), handmade paper that incorporates tiny sequins was used as gift wrap. Sheer ribbon was topped with velvet ribbon, wrapped around the box, and glued in place underneath. A gift tag cut from decorative paper was attached with a narrow organza ribbon bow to finish. Gift tags are a good way to add interest. Here (above right), a simply wrapped gift was dressed up with a label cut from handmade paper and a dainty felt flower adorned with a tiny pearl bead.

perfectly trimmed Dress up gifts with any scraps of braid and trim you have to hand. Here (below left) short lengths of ribbon and rickrack braid were embellished with mother-of-pearl buttons and wrapped around the corner of a present to create an irresistibly pretty effect. If you're giving two or three gifts, it looks elegant and sleek to coordinate the wrapping by using the same trim on each (this page). If it's a ribbon that also appears on the gift inside, so much the better!

new-baby cards

Decorate simple cards with motifs inspired by
the projects in the book—using buttons, bows, and
lace—to create the perfect finishing touch for your
precious handmade gifts.

cute as a button This cute card is the
perfect accompaniment to the photo album shown
on pages 96–99. It's also a good way of using up
any photo transfer paper left over from the project.
Follow the manufacturer's instructions to transfer
your chosen image to a plain white card, then let it
cool. Glue or sew the buttons all the way around the
photograph, then use a further dab of glue to attach
a tiny ribbon bow below the picture to finish.

initial thoughts This simple yet effective technique (left) uses a large needle to prick holes through the card. Draw baby's initial in soft pencil and prick the holes. When the initial is complete, erase the pencil marks. Now glue a length of lace or ribbon down one side of the card and finish with two buttons and a tiny silk ribbon bow.

happy heart Iron a square of fusible web to the back of a piece of pink gingham fabric and draw a heart shape on the wrong side (right). Cut out the heart, peel off the backing paper, and iron it to the center of a plain white card. Finish by gluing a natty pink ribbon bow to the top of the heart. This idea works well with any pretty fabric scraps.

blanket stitch

Blanket stitch is usually worked in wool to finish the raw edge of wool fabrics or blankets. It's a pretty, decorative stitch that's useful for creating a bold outline. Use tapestry or knitting yarn for this stitch, although it can also be worked in thicker thread like pearl cotton.

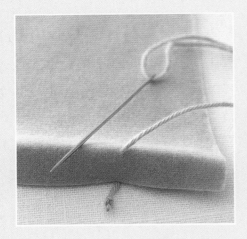

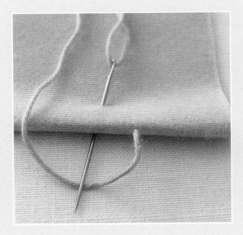

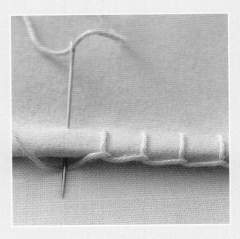

1 Fold up the raw edge of the fabric approximately ½in (1cm) to the inside. Press in place, if preferred. Now push the needle through the fabric from the wrong side, so it emerges from the folded crease. Carefully pull the needle all the way through.

2 Next, insert the needle through the front of the fabric, approximately ½in (1cm) along from the previous stitch. Bring the needle out through the fold of the hem, with the thread looped below the point of the needle. Pull the thread all the way through.

3 Repeat the stitch, always remembering to loop the thread below the point of the needle to create the blanket stitch. Take care not to pull the thread too tight. Always keep the stitches evenly spaced. It's best not to have them too far apart.

cross stitch

This stitch is worked in two parts and is great for filling in large expanses, such as the cross-stitch picture on pages 100-101. It's possible to buy woven fabric (sold under the names Aida or Evenweave) with holes spaced especially for cross stitch. Alternatively, you can use fabrics with woven or printed designs of squares or checks such as gingham.

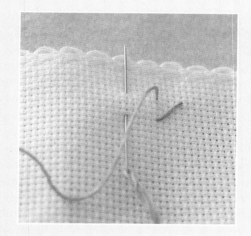

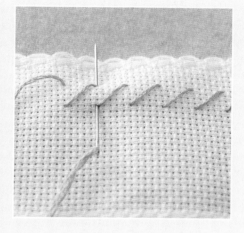

1 Cross stitch is generally worked in rows. Knot your thread and push the needle through from the back of the fabric to the front. Make a diagonal stitch downward from right to left, then push the needle back up to the top of the line of embroidery. Repeat for the desired length.

2 When the length of the first line is completed, the stitch is reversed to form the distinctive crosses that give the stitch its name. Pass the needle back across the first stitch on a diagonal, from left to right. Push the needle through the fabric at the bottom of the line of embroidery to form an X.

3 Continue to pass the needle neatly and evenly through the fabric on a diagonal, until you have formed an entire row of cross stitches. Repeat the process until you have built up the desired number of rows of cross stitch.

french knots

French knots are a simple and effective way of adding decoration.
They work best on flat fabrics. If you're working French knots on thicker
fabric, such as terrycloth, you may wish to work two or three of them in
one area so they are more visible.

 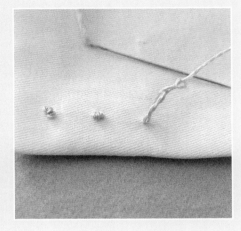 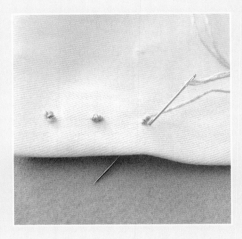

1 Thread the needle with two strands of embroidery floss. Push the needle all the way through the fabric from the back to the front side. Pulling the thread taut, wind it tightly around the needle three or four times.

2 Push the needle into the fabric close to where you brought it out. Lay down the needle. As you carefully pull the thread through the fabric, gently ease the twisted strands downward. As they come to rest on the fabric, they should form the shape of the knot.

3 Now stitch once over the knot to secure it and hold it in place. Repeat as necessary until you have made the desired number of knots.

chain stitch

This is a simple decorative stitch that can be used to work both straight and curved lines. If you are working curved shapes, smaller stitches are best. Single chain stitch can be used to create shapes such as the flower petals on the heart pillow (pages 92–95).

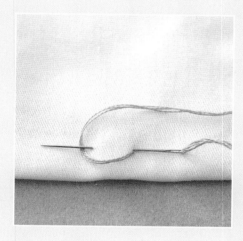 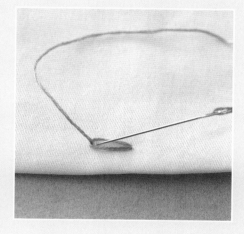 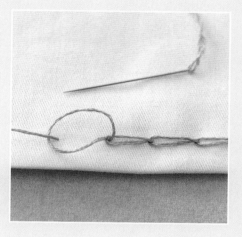

1 Knot your thread and push the needle through from the back of the fabric to the front. Make a stitch of ½in (1cm) and loop the thread around and under the needle's point.

2 Carefully pull the needle all the way through the fabric to form the loop of the chain stitch. Pull the thread through firmly and evenly. Try to keep the tension even, to keep the stitching from becoming too tight.

3 To make the next chain stitch, push the needle through the front of the fabric inside the loop of the chain and right beside the place where the needle came out. Now repeat step 1. Continue to the end, anchoring the last loop with a short stitch.

templates

The outlines shown on pages 116–121 have been reduced in size so they fit on these pages. Before cutting out the templates, enlarge them on a photocopier by 200 percent to make them the right size.

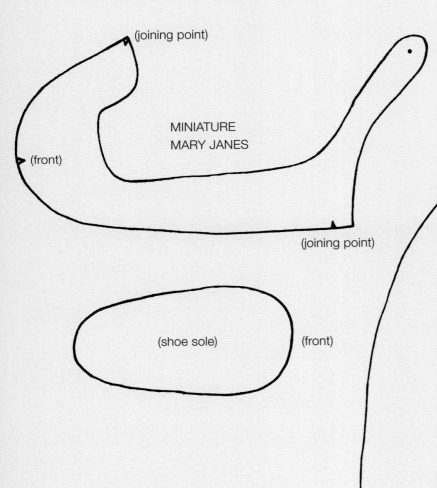

(joining point)

(front)

MINIATURE
MARY JANES

(joining point)

(shoe sole)   (front)

KNOTTED PIXIE HAT

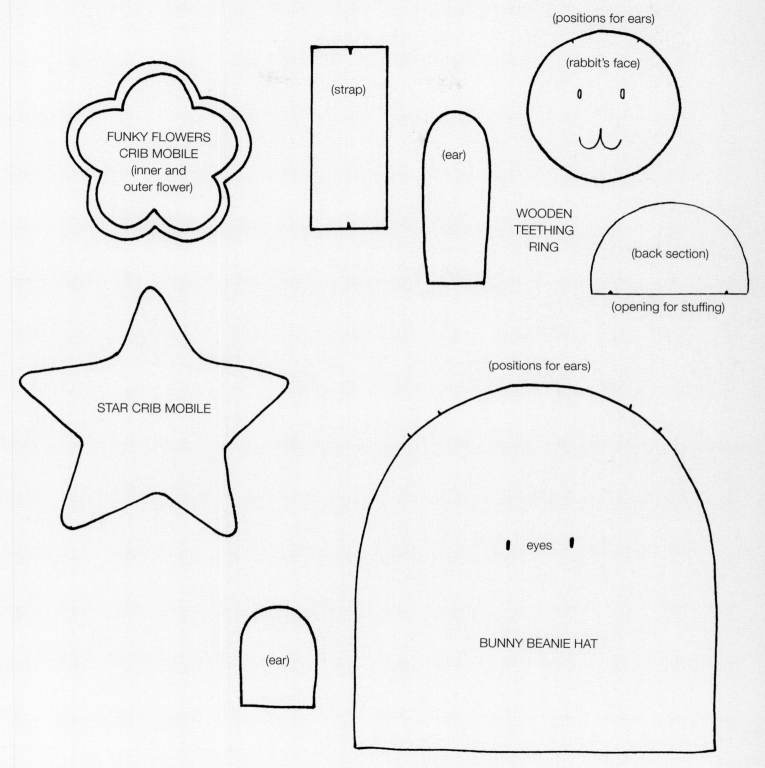

FUNKY FLOWERS
CRIB MOBILE
(inner and
outer flower)

(strap)

(ear)

(positions for ears)

(rabbit's face)

WOODEN
TEETHING
RING

(back section)

(opening for stuffing)

STAR CRIB MOBILE

(positions for ears)

eyes

BUNNY BEANIE HAT

(ear)

All templates must be
enlarged on a photocopier
by 200 percent to make
them the right size.

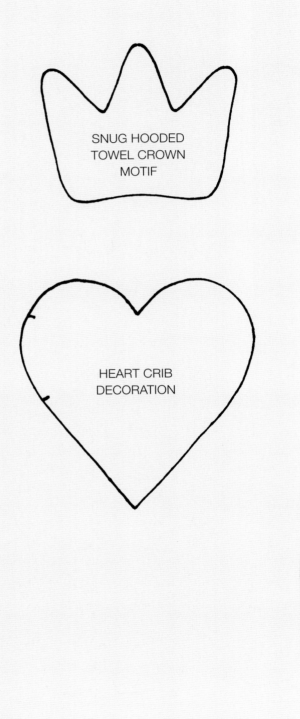

SNUG HOODED
TOWEL CROWN
MOTIF

alternative embroidery motifs
for BEST-DRESSED BIB

HEART CRIB
DECORATION

bottle motif
for bib

(place on fold of fabric)

BEST-DRESSED BIB

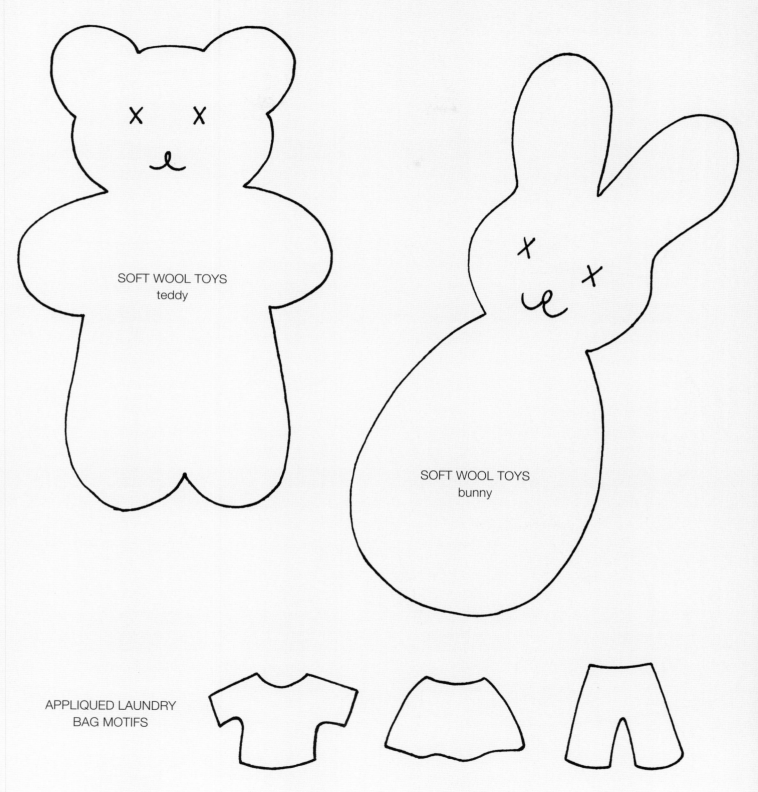

SOFT WOOL TOYS
teddy

SOFT WOOL TOYS
bunny

APPLIQUED LAUNDRY
BAG MOTIFS

MOTIFS FOR PRETTY
PATCHWORK BLANKET

All templates must be
enlarged on a photocopier
by 200 percent to make
them the right size.

HAND-EMBROIDERED
PILLOW

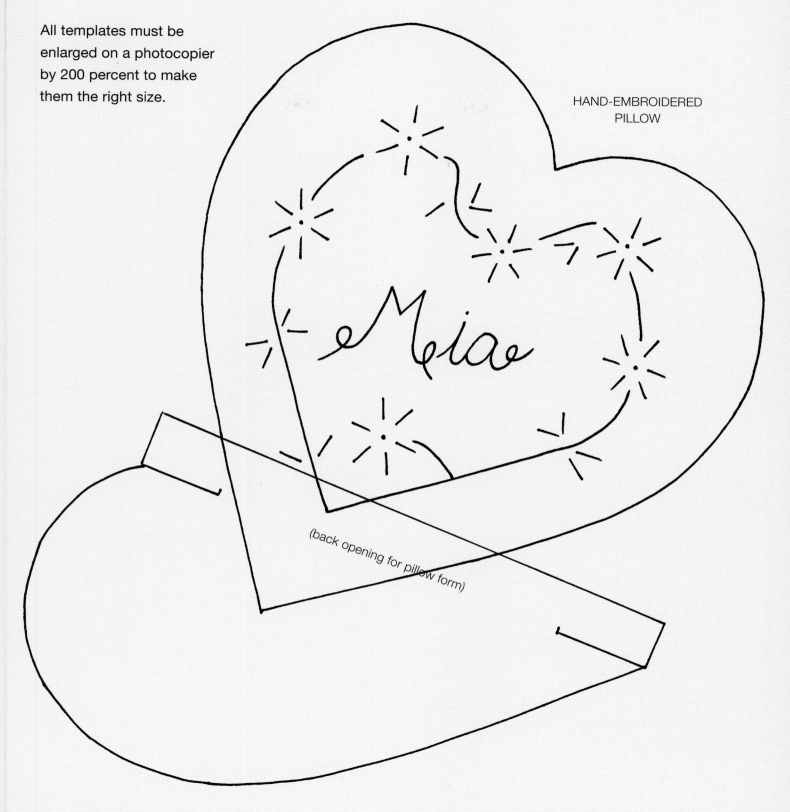

Mia

(back opening for pillow form)

sources

BABIES "R" US
Visit www.babiesrus.com or
call (800) BABY RUS for a
retailer near you.
*Complete line of linens for babies,
including simple and inexpensive
blankets and sheets and pure
cotton onesies and sleepsuits that
can be customized. Some simple
children's furniture, including plain
white toy chests and chairs that
can be painted.*

BABYSTYLE.COM
Visit www.babystyle.com or
call 877-378 9537 for a catalog.
*Simple, pretty nursery bedding
and accessories as well as soft
cotton clothing basics in cute
patterns.*

BRITEX FABRICS
146 Geary Street
San Francisco, CA 94108
415-392-2910
www.britexfabrics.com
*Huge variety of furnishing
fabrics, pretty ribbons, trims,
and other notions.*

**THE BUTTON EMPORIUM
& RIBBONRY**
914 S.W. 11th Avenue
Portland, OR 97205
503-228-6372
www.buttonemporium.com
*Vintage and assorted buttons
and ribbons, including adorable
mother-of-pearl buttons in duck,
star, flower, and rabbit shapes.
Also vintage trims, velvet ribbon,
and fringing with cute baby motifs
such as bees, bunnies, and ducks*

CATH KIDSTON
www.cathkidston.com
*Cheerful florals, polka-dots, and
retro-printed cottons that are great
for appliqué. Their vintage-style
furnishing fabrics include a circus,
jungle animals, sailing boat, and
cowboy prints.*

CITY CRICKET
215 W 10th St
New York, NY 10014
212-242-2258
www.citycricket.com
*Cute white-painted miniature
Adirondack chairs that can be
painted and customized.*

CRAFTING DIRECT
www.craftingdirect.com
*All kinds of essential crafting
equipment: sewing machines,
cross-stitch kits, cards and
papers, white glue, bumper packs
of sequins and beads, and more.*

DICK BLICK ART MATERIALS
Visit www.dickblick.com for
details of your nearest store.
*A Dick Blick store is an Aladdin's
cave of art and craft supplies.
They carry cold-water fabric dyes,
stenciling equipment, felt, and
cutting tools such as pinking
shears.*

FOAM SOURCE
1-800-255-0181
www.foamsource.com
Foam custom-cut to size.

GARNET HILL
Visit www.garnethill.com or
call (800) 870 3513 for a catalog.
*Baby clothing in soft natural fibers
and colorful, high-quality crib
bedlinen, including cotton Oxford
blankets and fleece throws that
can be appliquéd and
embroidered. Visit the website for
details of their outlet stores.*

**HEART OF THE HOME
STENCILS**
www.stencils4u.com
*Alphabet stencils as well as other
simple designs for kids.*

HYMAN HENDLER & SONS
67 West 38th Street
New York, NY 10018
212-840-8393
www.hymanhendler.com
*Novelty and vintage ribbons in
many different colors and designs.*

IKEA
Call 800-254-IKEA or visit
www.ikea.com for the location
of your nearest store.
*Kids' furniture, including unpainted
natural wood chairs and tables.
Also wooden photo frames, kids'
bedding, and cute accessories.*

JOANN FABRICS
Locations nationwide.
Visit www.joann.com for details
of your nearest store.
*Art and crafts supplier offering
sewing machines, thread, fabric,
cross-stitch kits, and more.*

KATE'S PAPERIE
561 Broadway
New York, NY 10012
212-941-9816
888-809-9880
www.katespaperie.com
*Stickers, stamps, paper punches,
and ribbons for gorgeous gift
wrapping.*

LAURA ASHLEY

Visit www.lauraashley-usa.com for a retailer near you.
Pretty vintage-style fabric as well as a selection of cute fabrics designed especially for babies' and children's rooms.

MICHAELS

Locations nationwide. Visit www.michaels.com for details of your nearest store.
A huge selection of every kind of art and craft material.

M&J TRIMMING

www.mjtrim.com
Fun and youthful trims for kids, including crocheted appliqués, teddy buttons, and pretty ribbons, all available online.

THE OLD FASHIONED MILK PAINT CO., INC.

436 Main Street
P.O. Box 222
Groton, MA 01450
978-448-6336
www.milkpaint.com
Non-fade colors including pretty nursery pastels.

PAPER SOURCE

www.paper-source.com
Simple, stylish crafting kits. Also envelopes, cards, and pretty handmade paper in a variety of designs, as well as crafting basics such as scissors, glue, and hole punches.

PAPER WISHES

888-300-3406
www.paperwishes.com
Good for card-making equipment, different kinds of paper, glue, stamps, and brushes.

PJ'S DECORATIVE FABRICS, INC.

511 West Broad Avenue
Albany, GA 31701
229-439-7265
www.pjsfabrics.com
Large selection of fabrics, including stripes, spots, and toiles. Also children's fabrics.

POTTERY BARN KIDS

Visit www.potterybarnkids.com for details of your nearest store.
Nursery bedding, including soft cotton blankets, plain wooden chairs that can be hand-painted for a new arrival, and a wide selection of storage baskets

RAG SHOP

1616 N. Federal Hwy.
Boca Raton, FL 33432
561-750-1196
Visit www.ragshop.com for details of their other stores.
Crafts store with huge selection of fabric, sewing accessories, and more.

REPRO DEPOT

www.reprodepot.com
This website is devoted to hard-to-find vintage style and retro-themed fabrics, buttons, and ribbons. It also offers quilt patterns and crafting kits for baby gifts.

THE RIBBONERIE

191 Potrero Avenue
San Francisco, CA 94103
415-626-6184
www.theribbonerie.com
Extensive collection of gorgeous ribbons, including adorable vintage French children's ribbons that are ideal for trimming blankets, laundry bags, or towels.

THE STENCIL LIBRARY

www.stencil-library.com
This UK-based site is the stockist of all the stencils shown in this book. Their children's stencils include traditional nursery-rhyme characters, marching soldiers, and Alice in Wonderland characters. Will ship to the United States.

STONE MOUNTAIN & DAUGHTER FABRICS

2518 Shattuck Avenue
Berkeley, CA 94704
510-845-6106
www.stonemountainfabric.com
This craft store offers fabric, yarn, notions, buttons, patterns, books, and even sewing classes.

TARGET

Locations nationwide
Visit www.target.com for details of your nearest store.
Baby bedding, nursery storage, baby layettes, and a plain white kids' slatback rocker that can be hand-decorated for a new baby.

TINSEL TRADING CO.

47 West 38th Street
New York, NY 10018
212-730-1030
www.tinseltrading.com
Selection of vintage buttons that would look perfect as decorative embellishments or attached to handmade cards. Also gingham and polka-dot ribbons and cute baby designs.

UTRECHT

Stores nationwide.
Visit www.utrechtart.com for details of your nearest store.
Craft essentials, including paintbrushes, glue, paper, and card.

picture credits

ALL PHOTOGRAPHY BY POLLY WREFORD

Page 1 hat fabric from John Lewis; page 2 wool blanket fabric from The Wimbledon Sewing and Craft Superstore; onesie from Mothercare; tapestry yarn from John Lewis; page 4–6 ribbon and rosettes from VV Rouleaux; embroidery thread and linen fabric from John Lewis; rattle stylist's own; lampshade from John Lewis; ribbon for bows from VV Rouleaux; cotton T-shirt fabric from MacCulloch & Wallis; embroidery thread from John Lewis; page 8–9 waffle fabric, embroidery thread and bias binding from John Lewis; high chair from IKEA; page 10–11 blanket and Moses basket from Mothercare; wool fabric, synthetic-fiber stuffing, cotton ribbon, and embroidery thread from The Wimbledon Sewing and Craft Superstore; page 12–13 as previous; onesie from Mothercare; page 14–15 cotton T-shirt fabric from MacCulloch & Wallis; embroidery thread and polka-dot background fabric from The Wimbledon Sewing and Craft Superstore; page 16–17 as previous; pink spot fabric for hat/onesie from Mothercare; page 18–19 velour and blue background fabric from The Wimbledon Sewing and Craft Superstore; shirt from Mothercare; embroidery thread and curtain ring from John Lewis; page 20–21 as previous; blue stretch terrycloth from John Lewis; page 22–23 blue stretch terrycloth and embroidery thread from John Lewis, polka-dot background fabric from The Wimbledon Sewing and Craft Superstore; page 24–25 pink wool fabric from The Wimbledon Sewing and Craft Superstore; pink polka-dot lining fabric and flower buttons from John Lewis; iron-on foam interfacing and bias binding from MacCulloch & Wallis; onesies from Mothercare; page 26–27 as previous; gingham fabric, star buttons, and snap fasteners from John Lewis; page 28–29 linen fabric and bias binding from MacCulloch & Wallis; embroidery thread from John Lewis; ribbon from VV Rouleaux; highchair from IKEA; page 30–31 as previous; page 32–33 paintbrushes from The Wimbledon Sewing and Craft Superstore; rattle stylist's own; shirt from Mothercare; page 34–35 floral fabrics from Cath Kidston, polka-dot fabric stylist's own; bells from The Wimbledon Sewing and Craft Superstore; foam cut to order by Foam For Comfort;

page 37 similar fabric available from Cath Kidston; page 38–39 terrycloth fabric, yellow fabric, bias binding, embroidery thread, and fusible web all from The Wimbledon Sewing and Craft Superstore; page 40–41 as previous; blue terrycloth for crown and piping cord from John Lewis; page 42–43 stencils from The Stencil Library; baby's top from John Lewis; page 44–45 blue polka-dot fabric from John Lewis; white polka-dot fabric and cotton ribbon from The Wimbledon Sewing and Craft Superstore; crib from IKEA; page 47 pink spot fabric, cotton ribbon, and synthetic-fiber filling from The Wimbledon Sewing and Craft Superstore; pink floral fabric from Cath Kidston; page 48–49 frame from IKEA, paint by Dulux; buttons and glue from John Lewis; page 50–51 frames from IKEA; paints by Dulux; buttons, glue, and fabric from John Lewis; letter cut to order by Action Graphics; page 52–53 letters cut to order by Action Graphics; paints by Dulux; paintbrushes from The Wimbledon Sewing and Craft Superstore; page 54–55 blankets from Mothercare; needlework band, fabric pen, and embroidery thread from The Wimbledon Sewing and Craft Superstore; page 56–57 blanket from Mothercare; fusible web, embroidery thread, and bias binding from The Wimbledon Sewing and Craft Superstore; floral fabric from Cath Kidston; page 58–59 white cotton fabric, motif fabrics, fusible web, ribbon, and needlework band all from The Wimbledon Sewing and Craft Superstore; buttons and cotton cord from John Lewis; clothes and blanket from Mothercare; page 60–61 white and blue polka-dot fabric, needlework band, and ribbon from The Wimbledon Sewing and Craft Superstore; blue polka-dot fabric and cord from John Lewis; star fabric from Cath Kidston; page 62 hangers from John Lewis; paints from Dulux; ribbons from Lakeland Ltd, baby shirt from Mothercare; page 64–65 star print fabric from Cath Kidston; cotton ribbon from The Wimbledon Sewing and Craft Superstore; similar basket from IKEA; page 67 pink fabrics from Cath Kidston; pink ribbon from V V Rouleaux; clothes from Mothercare; page 68–69 felt and buttons from John Lewis; synthetic-fiber stuffing and cotton tape from The Wimbledon Sewing and Craft Superstore; page 71 blue felt and star buttons from John Lewis; cotton ribbon as previous, crib from IKEA; page 72–73 wooden lamp base, lampshade, and buttons from John Lewis; paints by Dulux; silk

ribbon from VV Rouleaux; page 74–75 blue waffle lampshade, white lampshade, buttons, lamp base, and rickrack braid from John Lewis; page 76–77 stencils and brushes from The Stencil Library; page 78–79 as previous; page 80–81 similar chair from IKEA, stencils from The Stencil Library; page 82–83 wool fabrics from The Wimbledon Sewing and Craft Superstore; tapestry yarn from John Lewis; page 84–85 as previous; page 86–87 similar chair from IKEA; paint from Dulux, stencils and stencil brushes from The Stencil Library; page 88–89 similar chair from IKEA; paints from Dulux; mauve polka-dot fabric from John Lewis; gingham ribbon from The Wimbledon Sewing and Craft Superstore; page 90–91 paint from Dulux; stencil from The Stencil Library; page 92–93 linen fabric from MacCulloch & Wallis; silk ribbon and rosettes from VV Rouleaux; embroidery thread John Lewis; gingham ribbon from Lakeland Ltd; page 94–95 as previous; page 96–97 photo album and lining paper from Paperchase; linen fabric and iron-on transfer paper from MacCulloch & Wallis; buttons from John Lewis; white ribbon from The Wimbledon Sewing and Craft Superstore; page 98–99 as previous; page 100–101 gingham fabric and embroidery thread from John Lewis; frame from IKEA; paint from Dulux; page 102–103 plate and paints from Brush & Bisque It; pink polka-dot background fabric from John Lewis; page 104–105 boxes and papers from Paperchase; ribbons from John Lewis and Paperchase; page 106–107 lace, ribbon, and trim from MacCulloch & Wallis; flower motifs, sheer ribbon, and buttons from John Lewis; paper from Paperchase; labels and gingham ribbon from Lakeland Ltd; page 108–109 paper from Paperchase; ribbons and trims from MacCulloch & Wallis; buttons and handmade paper from John Lewis; cotton and gingham ribbons from The Wimbledon Sewing and Craft Superstore, flower and silk ribbon from VV Rouleaux; page 110–111 blank cards from John Lewis and The Wimbledon Sewing and Craft Superstore; buttons from John Lewis; gingham fabric, lace, and ribbon trim from MacCulloch & Wallis; pink ribbon from VV Rouleaux; page 112–113 wool fabric and embroidery cloth from The Wimbledon Sewing and Craft Superstore; thread and yarn from John Lewis; page 114–115 fabrics and thread from The Wimbledon Sewing and Craft Superstore; page 126 letters cut to order by Action Graphics.

index

acknowledgments

Thank you to Polly Wreford for her beautiful photography and her way of getting all the babies to smile so sweetly! All the pictures are stunning. Thanks also to Sonya Nathoo and Annabel Morgan for their help with all stages of the book—the design, layout, and words.

Thank you to all the cute babies who modeled, and to their patient mothers. And thank you to the Stencil Library, for supplying the stencils for many of the projects.

Finally, a big thank you to my husband Michael for his unfailing support, and to my daughters Jessica and Anna for their ideas and inspiration for the book.

Ryland Peters & Small would like to thank all the babies who modeled for this book, including Barnaby, Chloe, Erin, Ethan, Lara, and Tallulah.